"I am standing in front of Her statue at Karnak. Sekhmet tells me to take the stethoscope from my pocket and place it on Her chest. *What stethoscope?* I wonder. But when I reach into my pocket, the instrument is there, and I place it against the statue. When I do, I feel—not cold stone, but the heat of a living body. I hear the rise and fall of Her breathing. She then tells me to place my hand over Her breast. I hold my breath. How dare I touch this Supreme Deity whom I love so much? She lightly taps the top of my hand and shows me where to rest my palm against Her chest. Again, I feel and hear the rhythmic beating of Her heart and the throb of Her pulse. Incredulity and devotion sweep through me. I am actually experiencing the Goddess' living heartbeat!

'I am alive,' She says, 'I am alive!'"

—Excerpt from a Sacred Dream in *Fire in My Soul*

FIRE IN THE SOUL

FIRE IN

THE SOUL

Finding the Divinity within Each of Us

HELENA JUDITH STURNICK, PhD

Wild Prairie Press | Naples | Florida

For information about this title or to order other books and/ or electronic media, contact the publisher:
Wild Prairie Press
Naples, Florida
WildPrairie.Press / FireintheSoulBook.com
contact@fireinthesoulbook.com

Library of Congress Control Number: 2017916999
ISBN: 978-0-9995256-0-9

Printed in the United States of America
Cover and Interior design by Concept West
Interior layout by 1106 Design

Bible quotations are American King James version (AKJV).

Cover image: painting by Sandra Stanton, artist in Farmington, Maine.

Cataloging-in-Publication data in process

PRAISE FOR *FIRE IN THE SOUL*

"The book is splendid—richly told, deeply evocative of HERSELF (Sekhmet) and in ways that I think Sekhmet would approve. . . . I especially like the way Dr. Sturnick weaves in teaching for the readers so that they may cross the great divide in local consciousness and touch into their archetypal realm. I know that she has a very important work here that will help in the dissolution of the veils between the worlds."

—**Jean Houston,** author of *A Mythic Life, The Search for the Beloved, The Wizard of Us,* and numerous other books

"Dr. Sturnick lays out a compelling case for understanding the very real interaction between the world of Spirit with our human dimension. I was struck by her clarity, heart and insight in describing not only her own amazing encounter with the ancient Goddess Sekhmet, but also her ability to guide the reader along a path of greater personal insight. Provocative and approachable, this is a groundbreaking book that gives readers an intimate look into the soul and its role in our lives. Well done!"

—**Meredith Young-Sowers,** DDiv, author of *Agartha: a Journey to the Stars; The Angelic Messenger Cards;* and co-founder of the Stillpoint Foundation and School

"Are you curious about the super-normal? Have you encountered events you can't explain? Then this insightful and down-to-earth book, written by an amazing woman, is just what you may be looking for."

—**Margaret Lobenstine,** author of *The Renaissance Soul*

"Thank you. Thank you. Thank you. I feel privileged Dr. Sturnick asked me to read her book; it is so much more than a book for me."

—**Barry Heerman,** PhD, author of *A Noble Life, Igniting Extraordinary Passion in Life and Work*

Helena Sturnick has crafted a luminous and enchanting narrative of her decades-long encounters with Sekhmet, Protector of Humanity and Goddess of Transformation. As we read the gems of ancient wisdom from this Goddess, we may well find ourselves transformed in our present moments and future hopes. *Fire in the Soul* is a gift of imagination and spirit.

—**Reynolds-Anthony Harris,** Professional Advisor
and Counselor to Foundations, Boards, Corporations,
Organizations, and Leaders; Co-Founder and Facilitator
of Lyceum Partners

"Fire in the Soul will thrill and inspire you as this brilliant author gives us a glimpse of what is possible if we are willing to open our hearts to the wisdom and loving kindness beyond what we know in this dimension."

—**Donna Daisy,** PhD, author of *Why Wait? Be Happy Now*

With admiration, respect, and affection,
this book is dedicated to two co-founders
of the Human Potential movement:

Dr. Jean Houston
my colleague and friend over many years,
and a visionary thinker in the exploration
of human consciousness. She ignited the passion
of many of us for the Possible Impossible;
and
Dr. Robert Masters
scholar and metaphysical seeker, who renewed
the knowledge of Sekhmet in the world and
lighted the path of many seekers to the spiritual
world of ancient Mysteries.

ADDITIONAL APPRECIATION

Numerous dear friends and colleagues contributed to the completion of this book. Some of them read and reread chapters. They suggested possible directions for the narrative, metaphysical resources, and scholarly books. They gave me unlimited moral support and believed in my capacity to do justice to this narrative. Some of them even came to believe in the energetic reality of Sekhmet. To each of the individuals listed alphabetically below, my most profound gratitude goes out to you.

My spouse, Gail Murphy, deserves special attention. Her support has been loving, generous, and unwavering, even when this narrative at times took over our lives.

I would also like to thank:

Mary Ellen Briel
Deb Bucci
Mary Cown, PsyD
Donna Daisy, PhD
Normandi Ellis, PhD
Martin Erdsneker, PhD
Bill Greaves
Antonia Hall
Reynolds Anthony Harris
Barry Heerman, PhD
Margaret Lobenstine
Barbara E. Metcalfe, PhD
Sr. Michelle Meyers, MSc, MThSc
Marie Olmstead
Sr. Kay O'Neil, MSc, MThSc
Helene Shik
Lisa Wroble
Meredith Young-Sowers, DDiv

AUTHOR'S NOTE

Throughout this narrative, I have employed many terms for the presence of the Sacred in our lives: God/dess, the Presence, the Source, Divine Being, the Force, Divine Energy, Universal Spirit, Sacred Intelligence, and so on. In doing so, my intention is to emphasize the ubiquity and omniscience of this Energy, as well as to make the point that there are thousands of names, not simply one, to designate the infinite Divine Energy within each of us.

FOREWORD

This is a marvelous book! When I started reading it, I couldn't put it down. But it is not for the faint of heart.

Helena Sturnick extends a bold and audacious invitation to those willing to summon the courage, intellect, heart, and soul to transverse the only journey of any consequence, the Mystical Journey. She at once brilliantly defines the terrain, and sets forth a detailed map describing her experiences and the navigational tools necessary to the journey. She was graced to do this, channeled dare I say, through the Egyptian Goddess Sekhmet.

The author beautifully knits together the scientific, historical, cultural, and psycho-spiritual threads of mysticism. She does this by providing a grounded, intellectual weaving in the background, with her visceral, transcendental relationship with Sekhmet in the foreground. The author of this book is not a remote bystander, rather she is the Real Deal. You feel Dr. Sturnick's very cellular presence in the words and the space between the lines.

The author combines the best of our contemporary lives and Unknown worlds with her gifts of intellect and heart. She understands the power of linking science and spirituality, since she herself embodies training as rigorous academician with her consciousness as numinous seeker. Who better to write this book? No one better.

In another life, over twenty years ago, I knew Dr. Sturnick as the president of the university where I served. Now seeing many renderings of Sekhmet, as I review her manuscript, I am astonished to see the amazing luminous presence of Sekhmet in Helena's very physical and spiritual being. It is uncanny.

This is more than a book to me.

Barry Heerman, PhD
Author, *Noble Purpose, Igniting Extraordinary Passion in Life and Work*

CONTENTS

INTRODUCTION

We are living in revelational times where communications with spiritual energies are acknowledged and reported with increasing frequency by numerous individuals, who react sometimes with awe, and occasionally with fear or ambivalence. A plethora of public accounts has emerged during the past decade alone. A soldier in Iraq reports a visitation from the venerable Goddess Sekhmet before battle. After a near-death experience, an esteemed neurosurgeon writes a book describing his encounter with the illumination and astonishing peace of a world beyond this one. A well-known scholar encounters the ghost of a dear friend who brings a message important to her life.

Numerous other esoteric events that have occurred, however, have not been written about or recorded, although they are equally as stunning or poignant. In workshops, book club discussions, informal conversations, and elsewhere, ordinary people like you and me are beginning to share their dreams, visions, and messages from mysterious Divine Presences. Perhaps you have had your own mystical encounters. If so, you are not alone.

I write this book now for a number of compelling reasons:

- To affirm and validate your experiences with the supernormal
- To explore with you the breadth of paranormal events, whatever forms they take: visions, dreams, full-body experiences, interactive communication, and so on
- To open doors for my readers to participate in the Zeitgeist, or spirit, of our time
- To suggest the meanings of these paranormal experiences as I understand them
- To normalize the extraordinary—to the degree that this is possible

- To suggest practical ways by which each of us can claim our own Mystical Self without fear, confusion, or shame
- To find in spiritual mysteries the meaning of compassion
- To encourage each of us to use these experiences to enlarge our higher consciousness

Revelational times indeed! These supernatural events and Sacred Entities Who appear to us often speak with voices of Divine power and authority, calling us to "Awake!" to our personal and global spiritual crises. They beckon us to amplify our consciousness, to find the actions—grand or mundane—which ignite our passion to heal ourselves and our planet. These are the compelling messages for today, for this moment, and for our life purposes. Each of us, whether consciously or not, is embarking on a journey, as the Sacred Dreams described in this narrative suggest. Glimpses of other dimensions and messages directed to our souls inspire our quests, which may be more urgent now than ever, as we face not only the moonless nights of our inner landscapes, but the perilous state of the world. This is not a religious narrative, but it is imbued with sacred intent. Finding the Divinity within each of us is the journey we are summoned to make: to discover the Source within so that we can act outside of ourselves.

Across the globe, individuals are experiencing startling dreams of Sacred Beings communicating both hope and caution. In seminars and discussion circles on a variety of spiritual topics, people from all walks of life speak of inexplicable occurrences, describing their encounters, including out-of-body and near-death events; they seek validation, catharsis, and understanding. Yet each of these individuals is searching for more than validation. They seek meaning within a human community that will understand these mysterious happenings as not only within the realms of possibility, but powerful enough to shift the paradigms of each of our lives.

Many individuals express a haunting sense that they were born with a Divine contract in which they agreed before birth to the mission and template of their earthly lives. These contracts with Divine Force are commitments to events, actions, people whom we will

encounter, and choices which can create our expanded consciousness. Reluctant at first, I now firmly believe that each of us has such
a contract. The challenge is that we do not recall the details of those
sacred agreements when we are born into this life; our journey then is
to discover spiritual meaning during the course of our existence here.
Our experiences of mysterious events may be a call to remember the
essence of that promise.

Many of us are now shocked alive by electrical metaphysical
experiences unlike anything we have felt or witnessed before, and
comprehending such events does not come easily. The modern Western
world does not encourage paranormal awareness, nor is it supportive
of such cross-dimensional realities. This is even more disconcerting
since our reactions to these occurrences are often ambivalent. Who
really wants to see, in the middle of the night, a nun sitting and rocking in the chair beside the bed? Who invites a powerful goddess to
claim them—or who requests a foretelling dream that is a portent of
a daughter's drowning death the next morning? All of these things
happened to a member of my family or to me. We have little frame of
reference to comprehend such unexpected events in our lives. Is it any
wonder that we may respond with terror, disbelief, suspicion, joy, or
any number of other emotions? Whatever the feelings are, something
astonishing is happening that cannot be dismissed or ignored.

To reframe our responses so that we can define the meaning of
paranormal events, we can remember that these occurrences do not
take place in a vacuum. Books like Robert Holden's *Shift Happens* and
filmmaker Jonas Elrod's television series *In Deep Shift* have attracted
enthusiastic readers and audiences. Oprah's *Super Soul Sunday* is a
super ratings hit; she metaphorically placed her hand over our hearts
and found our beating pulses; she captured us with her interviews
with Deepak Chopra, Wayne Dyer, Joan Chittister, Caroline Myss,
Maya Angelou, and other women and men who have wisdom to share
with us. These spiritual thinkers affirm what many of us are already
perceiving as a new experiential system: a significant reality shift. We
are all part of a contemporary Zeitgeist, as the mood, beliefs, and ideas
of our age are changing radically. Simultaneously, numbers of us are

having our own uniquely moving spiritual experiences that reshape our intellectual and emotional landscapes.

You might be astonished to know how many prominent leaders, teachers, medical practitioners, and individuals in powerful positions—as well as the rest of us—are receiving a variety of mystical experiences. The validity of these occurrences (as discussed in Chapter 1) is reinforced by ongoing discoveries in the New Sciences (physics, neurobiology, neurology, brain research, mathematics) that are rapidly creating new realities of faith and culture. Although some people may still view these experiences askance, such events offer new possibilities for profound connections with our inner Divinity. Perhaps we are now truly on the brink of accessible intimacy with the Sacred.

In my own case, and over the course of my life, recurrent mystical events flipped me over in mental and spiritual somersaults. This narrative relates my journey that began when I was two years old. It has continued throughout my life, including my connection with a mysterious and powerful ancient Goddess who has been present to me for the past twenty years: Sekhmet, the lion-headed Divinity Who is a sacred source of healing and protection for the human race, as well as the creator of Magic (manifestation by a different name). Perhaps one of the most ancient God-Beings, Sekhmet now summons many of us to know Her sacred teachings and to do Her Divine work. For two decades, She has guided me. Although you may not resonate to her particular Presence, She is a template for the working of Divine Energy in each of our lives. This narrative can be instrumental in your discovery of your own inner Presence, by whatever name that Power is known to you.

Thirty-five years ago, I did not believe the concepts I now write about with such commitment. I was dismissive of the numerous strange events in my life until I could no longer deny them. Why were these Spirit visits, dreams, and waking visions happening to me? I soon learned that I was not alone. As I exchanged my stories with numbers of other individuals at conferences, workshops, over afternoon coffees, through interviews, and via Internet, my conviction deepened that spiritual guides, messengers, God/dess Beings were reaching out to us, sending us these phenomena. Consequently, we are living through, and witnessing, an explosion of startling esoteric events.

This is not only my story; each of us has our own mysterious tales. The Reflections at the end of each chapter are intended to bring the chapter content home to your mind and heart. Responding to those questions will deepen your understanding and assist your expanding consciousness. What we read has meaning to the extent that we can relate it to our own lives and allow the narrative's intent into our individual spiritual stories. Each of us is a participant in the shifting realities catalyzing many spiritual seekers to discover the luminous Divinity within. Any one of us is capable of receiving experiences from other realms or dimensions at any point in our lives. Such experiences do not merely happen to other people—they happen to us.

Helena Judith Sturnick, PhD

INVOCATION

This book presents the Divine and Universal Spirit of the powerful, mysterious, most ancient Goddess Sekhmet,

Who blesses now
The intentions
Words and images
Visions and dreams
Love and faith
Illuminated in these pages, and
Whose profound Presence is revealed here.
The Great Lady's fire, passion and energy
Blazes with the Spirit of our time,
As She has ignited every age of timeless time
With innovation, change, multi-dimensionality, and creativity.
This book transcribes the fascination and awe
She inspires, and
Her transformative Force in the World.

This Work is now consecrated by Her.

Sekhmet blesses this book.

CHAPTER ONE

The Statue
with the Breath of Life

In a heartbeat, the sacred statue of Sekhmet came alive. I held my breath as I stood in the small side room at Karnak.

"At last you have come home to Me, My Daughter," said the great Goddess Sekhmet, Her eyes huge and luminous as She gazed at me. Goosebumps appeared on my arms, and a cold shiver rippled up my spine.

Standing alone in the silence of the semi-dark room during a warm Egyptian afternoon at the end of Ramadan, the scuffed and hard-packed dirt floor beneath my feet, I was mesmerized by Her seven-foot, standing statue. Carved of black diorite, She held the traditional papyrus staff in Her left hand and the symbol of infinity in Her right. On Her head rested the circle of the sun, in the center of which was a rearing cobra, a symbol of Divine Wisdom and prophesy. A tall, narrow window, set high against the back wall of rough granite blocks, let in just enough light to see by. Dust motes lazily swirled in that stream of pale light, while the sweet scent of jasmine drifted in from the outside.

Her all-encompassing energy, radiating from the statue, filled the space. I felt calm and anticipatory at the same time. As Her spiritual force surrounded me, my heart throbbed. Every one of my senses was on high alert to absorb every particle of this experience. My senses

Sekhmet Statue at Karnak **(following page):** The image that came alive in my presence is a phenomenon reported by many others over several decades. The intensity of the experience has been described by those who receive it as "swooning," "transcendence," "all-encompassing love and compassion," and similar expressions. Photo of statue at Karnak by author, 1995.

I

merged, doubled, and tripled in intensity. I could smell and taste the earthen floor simultaneously, could hear a sound and see the color vibrating from it at the same time. The sensation of every nerve in my body was amplified.

I stood in sacred space.

As She spoke to me again, a template of the carved figure seemed to rise from the stone, a translucent duplicate of the statue. Waves of vibrant energy rose, creating an ineffable essence that I could not name or describe. The statue itself did not move or walk around, yet it was alive, "inspirited" with Divine Presence.

Sekhmet's immense, luminous eyes transfixed me then, and, many years later, the memory transfixes me still. All wisdom, consciousness, and eternity smoldered in those eyes. Looking into them was like being absorbed into infinity. In the depth of Her eyes, She was so *alive*.

She repeated Her words: "At last you have come home to Me, My daughter."

In the true presence of the Living Goddess, I was unable to move or speak. Her absolute authority and power without end stopped me in my tracks. The warmth of Her words flowed through me. Suddenly the earth, the stone walls, the statue itself, and all things tangible fell away. There was no longer a separate *me*. Body and ego did not exist—there was only Sekhmet's powerful energy in an infinite space filled with swirls and points of light.

As my ego dissolved, my energy merged into Hers. I *became* Her, in Her and of Her; we were the same essence. I became pure consciousness in a realm where time and space no longer existed. Enveloped in Her profoundly loving energy, I was paralyzed with awe. This was a force that the ordinary dimensions of reality absolutely could not encompass. Nothing in my life, reading, or experience could have prepared me for this. The fact is that such an experience is beyond words or descriptions.

Transported by this ancient Goddess into the center of the moving universe, I was a particle in the infinite stream of all consciousness. Consumed by the wonder of Her presence, I loved and adored Her beyond any human conception of these words. I was divinely enthralled—a common reaction of those who are "taken" by a God-Being.

Reacting to the Sacred

This Mystery occurred at the great Temple of Karnak, Egypt, in a small room where a single statue of Sekhmet resides.

Writing this now, years later, I pause. Although the language may seem overblown to a reader, the words cannot express the feelings evoked by this Divine Presence. Capturing the high velocity of the emotions still eludes me. The experience, exquisite and yet shattering, transformed my soul and my life. With a cellular consciousness that I don't comprehend even now, I knew that I had adored and served Sekhmet through many lives over thousands of years. Karnak was not our first meeting. I *knew* Her in my bones, my brain, and my blood. As I am recounting this now for the reader, the impact of Her Divine magnificence still shocks my entire being.

So this was the experience of being in the Presence of the Living God! As is not uncommon in such mystical events, terror and wonder were intertwined.

Finally, Sekhmet brought me back to ordinary reality, and I again felt the ground beneath my feet.

"Now," She said as I shook my head to clear it, "what would you ask me, My Daughter?"

Mind blank, and still in the grip of the inexplicable events, I did not know what to ask. A few words came at last.

"What happens next?" It was a question I have often asked Her over ensuing years.

"You are safe, and you are blessed."

"What is my Mission?"

"Do My work."

"Will you tell me more?"

"Your life is changing. Trust what is to come."

There had been such dynamic intimacy during the merging of our energies that now I was filled with the human need to touch Her.

"Place your hand on my staff," She said.

With trepidation that I might be burned up by the force of Her energy, I made myself cross the few feet of space between the statue and me. My physical body felt as if it no longer fit me as I raised my shaking hand to place it on top of the cool, smooth papyrus staff.

Once more, I was flooded with a love so intense I thought I might dissolve at Her feet.

"Thank you," I said. "Thank you."

Bowing myself out of the dark room, I walked unsteadily into the fierce Egyptian afternoon sun; into the scents of jasmine, lotus, and seductive honeysuckle; and into the chattering circle of my sister travelers. I had not stopped trembling. Stepping back into daily reality seemed an impossibility. All my spiritual and reality paradigms had seismically shifted; my interior landscape was altered forever.

To my surprise, I started to weep gulping, body-wracking tears that wouldn't stop. Like a disoriented animal, I sought a lair to burrow into. Stumbling among the broken rocks, I found a half-wall I could lean against as I slipped to the ground. Melting bonelessly against that crumbling structure, I pulled my legs up against my body, holding myself, rocking and crying with relief, wonder, and confusion. The bright and noisy world seemed too strong after the silence of the Mystery.

My dearest friend, Marie, came to sit beside me, silently easing me into her arms. She held my shaking body for a long time. A metaphysical teacher, she understood that this was a normal reaction to an abnormally intense spiritual experience. Repeating a reassuring mantra, she murmured, "It's all right; sh-h-h, you will be all right."

It was more than an hour before I knew that I would be.

Awakening in Reality

This description may seem like a hysterical reaction to the Sekhmet experience. In fact, crying and physically shaking are typical human reactions to profound mystical happenings. As researchers and psychologists have found, these physical responses are classic characteristics of one of the stages of Mysticism: the process of "Awakening to the Mysteries." In a later chapter, I will discuss sacred Mysteries and Mystery Schools at greater length. In the meantime, these observations remind us that this narrative describes my supernormal contacts, as I experienced them. The comments are an aid to understanding your own exposure to the mysterious and to help you place them in a context of realities beyond the fixed dimensions we have been taught.

Despite this, the power of Sekhmet's appearance when I was age fifty-four astonished me. Although I had been intrigued, both as a scholar and a seeker, by the Egyptian Pantheon, I was absolutely not drawn to animal-headed gods or goddesses. Such Divine Beings had emerged, I assumed, before the greater sophistication of contemporary thinking and were now merely an interesting curiosity for research. The experiences with Sekhmet, however, have demonstrated that the imaginative countenance of God-Beings is simply a means of visualizing Divine Energy embodied in human form. What we see externally, we can also perceive in our interior minds.

How did I end up in Egypt and why did I travel there? Because Sekhmet called me to Her.

Twenty years ago, friends persuaded me to enroll with them in a ten-day residential Mystery School (Mystery: that which God alone knows that humans cannot know) held at a secluded location on Purple Mountain in Vermont. One afternoon, near the end of the workshop, as I was engaged in a walking meditation in the woods, a pale white light filtered through the dense trees. In a rush of energy, the shadowy, blurry figure of a lion-headed goddess manifested. At first it was so vague that I scarcely saw it. Then I heard a voice—not exterior to me, but in my head.

"I am Sekhmet, powerful and mighty. Come to Egypt," She commanded. Not only had Sekhmet not been on my mind, but Her image did not intrigue me. I turned to walk away.

6

Such was a scenario that would be repeated between us many times during the next year. She would invite me to come to Her—and I would flee from Her. Why, then, did She seek me? I wanted a God figure with a human face, like Isis or Artemis, as my guide. How egocentric to believe that I—or any of us—have real choices in these matters! The Mysteries come to us as they will. Our gratitude should be enormous that we are allowed into the sphere of Divine Energy, whatever form it takes.

"Come to Egypt!" Sekhmet repeated. There was no mistaking the directive; refusing was not an option. *Feeling* the energetic force of Her tone, I finally got it.

"Okay. I will come to Egypt," I promised. "I don't understand why you have called me, and I don't know how I'll get there. But I *will* find a way."

The Goddess acknowledged my words with a slight dip of Her head, as I perceived it. Nothing more was needed.

Fulfilling a Promise

When I described Sekhmet's appearance to our Mystery School teacher, Helene, she said, "How lucky you are! I could take you to Egypt. I was finished leading trips there; it's too dangerous now. But I believe in a command from Sekhmet; it's a sign for me, too. We'll go to Egypt."

True to Helene's word, a small group of us landed in Cairo seven months later, right after Ramadan.

Aftermath of Sekhmet's Appearance

Later that afternoon, following my experience with Sekhmet's statue, Marie and I took a walk through the cacophonous streets of Luxor (across the river from the site of Karnak). As usual, my beautiful companion attracted a long tail of Egyptian men who tried to get her attention. The scene was a stark incongruity to the silent, shadowed room at Karnak. Thousands of years of sacred history now collapsed into the frenzied activity of contemporary streets.

"Why Sekhmet? Why now?" I asked Marie as we strolled down one of the long streets.

"We don't choose these events," Marie said. "When they occur, we accept them and try to figure out the meaning. I wouldn't worry about it—Sekhmet is going to stay with you."

"How do you know?"

"Honey," she rolled her eyes after a long pause, "*think* about what just happened!"

Marie was right, of course.

Divine Presence

When Sekhmet called me to Egypt, She had—as She always does—a definite purpose. Significantly, these initial occurrences with Sekhmet happened at Karnak, a series of three temples constructed by Amenhotep III on the east bank of the Nile near Thebes (now the modern city of Luxor). This was the center of Sekhmet worship in Ancient Egypt, especially prevalent in the Nineteenth and Eighteenth Dynasties. There are over 700 statues of the Goddess still extant there, although many of them are now rubble. On this site, Her priestesses conducted daily rituals in Her honor, performed before different statues each day so that each figure was duly honored.

This is also the only remaining temple site that may have been solely administered by priestesses and other women. The Sacred Feminine presence held sway in politics and religion there. In addition, scholars believe that the Ka—or soul essence—of Sekhmet was inspirited in one of the main statues, most likely the carved figure I encountered. That statue had similarly intrigued the metaphysical scholar, Dr. Robert Masters, who had performed a ritual, inspiriting invocation a few years earlier, when he had called Her soul into the granite figure at Karnak. You will learn more about him later when I describe his mentoring role in my life.

Although we may not now be familiar with Sekhmet, She once held immense sway over the politics and priestly functions of Egyptian rulers. The best illustrations of Her authority are represented by the reigns of Queen Hatshepsut (ruling from approximately 1473-1458, BCE) and Amenhotep III (ruling from either 1390-1352 or 1388-1351, BCE). When the powerful Queen Hatshepsut (perhaps one of the most effective women leaders in history) ascended to the throne in the Eighteenth Dynasty, she aligned herself with Sekhmet, particularly with the Goddess' strength, courage, power and protection. As a result, the Queen established sacred festivals and magic rites honoring this Goddess.

Several decades after Hatshepsut's successful reign, Amenhotep III ascended to the throne. Like the venerable Queen before him, he aligned himself with Sekhmet. A ruler plagued with ill health, he revered Sekhmet's role as healer, Lady of Magic, and protector. In devotion to Her, he erected more than 760 statues, a number large enough to accommodate daily worship at his temple of two Sekhmet statues—one seated and one standing—each day of the year. Recent excavation of his funerary temple in 2013 uncovered sixty-four additional statues of all sizes, more evidence of Her ubiquitousness. The site has become, as a consequence of this long history of veneration, saturated with the immanence of the Sacred. Contemporary village women still clandestinely visit Sekhmet statues at night, performing secret fertility ceremonies. Sekhmet's mystical Divinity has not only radiated across eons of time and culture, but Her image still burns into human consciousness—from the scholars who seek to explain Her lost history, to those who have been seized by Her, to the village women with their petitions and offerings.

The living statue I encountered at Karnak is iconic. Believers in Her presence—and even some skeptics who have visited the site—speak of "swooning" at the energy the statue embodies. Of course Sekhmet called me to this place where I would meet Her in that magical environment, imbued with Her power. Experiencing the aura of mystery there and absorbing the Goddess's Sacred Presence has been, and still remains, an essential aspect of my personal understanding of Her and the esoteric. Although the tales about Her often describe her role in events of war and destruction, in Egyptian lore She is also a great healer and the founder of Temple Magic, the foundation of the healing arts. So significant was Her power that no healing rites were conducted without the presence of a priest of Sekhmet, a validation of Her preeminence, as well as Her restorative power.

Comprehending the Karnak Experience

A few days after the Karnak encounter, my group returned home. Coming to grips with the aftermath of this experience was going to be—no surprise!—a process as complex as the Goddess Herself. The next few months were a time of psychic decompression and decoding the meaning of the Egyptian experience. It was also a space for meditating on the relentless and ecstatic journey Sekhmet offered, which was really a journey into myself. She was challenging me to summon the spiritual courage to accept Her presence as the essence of my own soul. I had begun to live out, literally and metaphorically, what would become my lifelong saga under Her tutelage.

As months passed, and late winter zigzagged into spring, I continued to grapple with my reaction to the Sekhmet encounter. The experience at Karnak shifted my creativity into high gear, and I wrote in my journal several times a day. Who was this Goddess, barely known by me, who had claimed me with such certainty? Of course, I also acknowledged to myself a continuing caution about the Karnak event. Was it a hallucination brought on by travel fatigue coupled with the unfamiliar scents, sounds, and sights of Egypt? Did I imagine it? How was it possible to experience something so sublime in our mundane world? Seeking to understand Her appearance in Egypt was not unlike falling passionately in love, yearning for greater knowledge of the mysterious Beloved.

Around the same time, strange dreams begun to occur, sparsely at first, and then in clusters. Metaphysical in content and theme, they featured Sekhmet as a key narrator and participant. As the dream sequences expanded, they revealed more about the nature of Sekhmet and Her significance in a Divine pantheon of Spiritual Beings. She came to me every day with indisputable, loving possessiveness, much to my consternation. There was no escaping Her; She had planted her flag in my psyche. Her persistent Presence overpowered everything else. Because I had no authentic frame of reference, I felt a terrible vulnerability. I had no idea what She expected of me, nor how to live at peace with Her power. The truth is, Her transcendent, fiery energy was too much *there*.

One morning after meditation, I said, "Great Sekhmet, I am terrified of You, and I can't go forward with You. Thank You—I am so grateful for the sacred experiences You have given me, but I don't know how to live with Your high-voltage energy."

This is not an unusual reaction to Divine Presence. In your own spiritual experiences, if you continue to seek direct paranormal encounters and/or if they come to you spontaneously, you may feel the same vulnerability as you stand in the gap between human and Divine realms.

I had hoped Sekhmet would release me with words of blessing, such as, "I understand; I will leave you in peace."

Never underestimate the tenacity of Sacred Beings. Of course, Sekhmet did not leave me in peace. For the first time, I realized that She and I were bound by a Sacred Contract that I needed to figure out on this plane. No one in any of my academic or social networks knew about, or had any particular interest in, mystical phenomena. I needed a knowledgeable mentor who could appreciate the immensity of this experience, as well as my contradictory emotions.

Preparing to Undertake a Spiritual Journey

In the fall, the members of my travel group gathered to share pictures of the Egypt trip and reminisce. All of us had bonded during the adventure (which had been dangerous enough to require armed guards in Jeeps preceding our bus in the countryside, especially in the Sinai Desert). The conscious spiritual journey undertaken by our cluster of thirteen people (a sacred number) had been affecting in different ways for each of us. When Helene, our group leader, walked into the room where we had gathered, she handed me a book by Robert Masters, titled *The Goddess Sekhmet.*

"I have never met Masters," she said, "but read this. It may help you. There is also contact information in the back."

I took the book with relief. Dr. Masters, an acknowledged scholar who had described his own experiences with the Goddess, could serve as a guide and sounding board. After I read the book, however, I felt even more strongly that I was not a spiritual match for this Goddess. In describing Her power, Masters had also addressed Her ferocity, tenacity and unbounded energy. Although similar terms might describe me, my characteristics are human, whereas Hers are magnified by the mystery of the Divine. Already spooked by my own imagination, I wanted to flee.

To compound the matter, he warned that the faint of heart should not attempt to follow Her. As I reread Masters' text, I had third, fourth, and fifth thoughts when he cautioned about the psycho-spiritual perils of proceeding on a journey with this Goddess. The initial section of Dr. Masters's book is titled, "Preface and Words of Caution." He makes this observation about the perils of working with Sekhmet:

> . . . *this book has the power to drastically change you, to alter your reality more or less extremely. If it leads deeply into the Fifth Way, then you will awaken to recognize that you have been living in a kind of demented dream, close to the edges of both madness and death. After that, you will need guidance in a world very strange to you, where wakefulness and sanity threaten to consume you with their radiance. If you are unwilling to risk transformation, then by all means set this book aside now.*
>
> *But if you decide to continue—the Words of Caution have been provided.*

Language so strongly stated cannot be brushed aside. A warning from a hierophant who dedicated his life to working with Sekhmet demands attention. His reference to the Fifth Way is to ancient traditions that define the five interactive dimensions in which every human being can participate in interplay with Sacred Energies. To achieve this condition, however, humans must develop a discerning consciousness that allows us to differentiate among each of these Five Bodies (which are also different realities of our Selves). In learning the Ways, we can attain a level of metaphysical skill that can manifest the seemingly impossible. To do so is to reach the mystical level of a Shaman or Wizard.

After thinking about his words, my ambivalence was, as you might expect, cautionary. What would the presence of this Sacred Being truly mean for my life? Sekhmet had already demonstrated that it entailed disruption, radical change, challenges, obliteration of Ego, along with indescribable love. Could I survive a life filled to the brim with such experiences? What is required to develop the necessary inner resources? What, indeed, does this mean for each of us who seeks profound spiritual understanding? After many years, I can tell you that our Divine resilience is greater than we ever imagined.

I had assumed that mine was a garden-variety mystical experience, in contrast to the more dramatic events that must have happened to others: Saint Joan, St. John of the Cross, Paul on the road to Demascus, Hildegard of Bingen, for instance. Absolutely wrong! There is no "garden-variety" Divine experience, and mine was indeed significant. Every esoteric event that occurs in your life is noteworthy; they are messages and Divine prompts.

Denying the Divine

A few days after the potluck, and after I had again read Bob's book, I was enjoying my morning silence when I felt the now-familiar electricity of Sekhmet's presence hovering near me. The hairs on my arms stood up. Drawing a deep breath, I told Her again:

"Gracious Lady, Your presence is an honor I do not deserve. Truthfully, You scare me to death! Thank You for showing me Your Divine presence, and forgive me for my fear. But please leave me alone!"

Like Peter denying Jesus, this was the second time I had turned away from Her. But I felt resolute in my refusal.

Three hours later, I was hurrying to have lunch with my mentor, Annie, a woman who had been to Egypt the year before I travelled there. Having experienced her own connection with the Goddess at Karnak, she had begun researching the history and myths of Sekhmet. In Annie's worldview, the energy of the Source takes many forms, all of them sacred. Sekhmet simply revealed a more highly charged vibration than many other God-forms display. Each of us is generally drawn to the energy that fits our nature and life purpose.

As I was vacuuming the kitchen floor, my mind focused only on the day's schedule, I again felt the familiar *swoosh* of energy around me. Dropping the vacuum hose, I turned slowly to *see* the shadowy form of Sekhmet filling the back part of the kitchen. All the air went out of me as I realized that I could no longer fight Her claim to my life.

I thought about Francis Thompson's haunting poem, "The Hound of Heaven." The poem's narrator is relentlessly pursued by the God-Force, the Hound of Heaven, who is running him to ground—just as I, too, was pursued by my Divine Being. Thompson's description of fleeing from a Force too powerful to be resisted was my story, too. (In quoting the lines, I have changed the male pronouns to feminine in order to better reflect my emotions around the Goddess's pursuit):

> *I fled Her, down the night and down the*
> *Days;*
> *I fled Her, down the arches of the years;*
> *I fled Her, down the labyrinthine ways*
> *Of my own mind; and in the mist of tears*
> *I fled from Her. . . .*
> *I am defenseless utterly. . . .*
> *She calls, Rise, clasp My hand, and come. . .*
> *I am Her Whom thou seekest!*

I lifted my hands in an open gesture; and I waited.

"I claim you!" She said with the utmost authority. "You are Mine and I claim you."

This was my spiritual pivot point. Simultaneously, I was both beaten to the ground and uplifted. Surrender was inevitable. Theologian and teacher Marianne Williamson's description of this phenomenon is pitch perfect:

> *Until your knees finally hit the floor, you're just playing at life, and on some level you're scared because you know you're just playing. The moment of surrender is not when life is over. It's when it begins.*

"Yes," I said as I surrendered completely. "Yes!"
And then my life began.

Reflections: Chapter One

"Surrender" was one of Sekhmet's earliest commands to me. The concept of abandoning myself completely to a powerful God-Energy continued the spiritual process of Annihilation of the Ego. For me, it was one of the most difficult actions I have ever taken; it meant giving up control and allowing Her direction to override my life. Every time I had tentatively surrendered at the beginning of our encounters, I reversed myself and tried to take back my will. However, as I now comprehend, God-Forces are sovereign over realms in which no half-measures are allowed.

1. Define *surrender* as you understand it in the context of your life.
2. What is the emotional freight of this word for you? Are you exhilarated at the thought of such action? Are you afraid of it? Are you turned off by the concept of giving up your will to supernatural power? Journal about your emotional reactions to surrendering. You may be surprised at what you uncover.
3. If you can envision "surrender," what stands between you and this spiritual action?

CHAPTER TWO

Science of the Soul

How do we make "sense" of the supernatural? Our reactions to the paranormal swing wide with emotions ranging from skepticism and outright rejection to mystical ecstasy.

Let me share an anecdote with you that captures our ambivalent responses. Recently, a discussion group invited me to present a morning seminar on Mysticism. This was a low-key opportunity to preview some of the materials from this book, as well as to hear reactions to the subject. At the conclusion of my introduction to the topic, the group—now turbocharged by the concepts and experiences I had presented—was eager for discussion.

"This isn't the way I think about Mysticism!" said a fortyish woman as she put her pen down on the notebook resting on her knee. "Very interesting. But maybe a little disturbing, too."

"Oh, I don't agree," one participant said to her. "I use similar spiritual concepts as the basis of my healing practice. So this doesn't seem at all strange to me—energy, Spiritual Presence during healing, the body-soul connection."

One of the younger group members jumped in. "You know, I've been reading about discoveries in the New Science—how everything is energy connected in one big web. I'm not real; you're not real—except as a cluster of vibrations."

"I'm not sure you've got it quite right, but whatever these new theories are—well, it shakes up everything we believe," the healer mused. "And quantum physics blows me away—I can't totally wrap my head around it."

"I don't know," another participant said with hesitant earnestness. "My grandmother had The Sight—that's what we called it. And she could tell all kinds of things about people and situations. That was way before this New Science stuff."

Another woman, quite agitated, now entered the conversation. "I, for one, don't believe one word of this: energy, vibrations, and ideas I don't understand and don't want to—although I think *she* believes it." She waved her hand dismissively in my direction. "Frankly, I fear for Helena's soul—in fact," she looked sharply at me, "I am terribly afraid for you. This—this story is just how Satan works! He takes on whatever disguise will seduce us, as I know he did with you!"

An observer, whom I knew to be a former nun, spoke up. "I am so glad that Beth just made her point about evil, but I have a different take on this. Helena has given me a lot to think about. For years I taught comparative religion, without feeling my boundaries were threatened. However, if all this is true, then many of my ideas are being challenged. These concepts may just be too revolutionary for most of us."

You might wonder what your reactions would have been following that meeting. My response, as I drove home, was to grapple with their concerns. How best should I address such questions and comments in this narrative, as well as in other public presentations? The woman who feared for my soul was sincere in her comments. For perhaps the first time, a realization sank into my bones that this could be one of the common reactions I might encounter about mystical realities. Many people, in fact, do not want their worldviews shifted or tampered with. Perhaps most of us do prefer comfortable faith, safe stories of miraculous events, rather than jolting new paradigms that may seem impossible, at least on the surface.

As an academic by profession, *thinking* about ideas, especially paradoxical ones, is what I do best. So when I reached home, I turned immediately to my library of recent books and publications on brain research, the New Physics, and associated ideas. The continuity and profundity of my own esoteric experiences left no doubt in my mind about mystical realities, ancient and modern. Now it was apparent, however, that my narrative needed the addition of an exploratory chapter on "The Science of the Soul"—scholarly research about the findings that are now tilting our paradigms with audacious knowledge, some of it new, and some amplifying information and practices the human race has known for millennia. (Mystical experiences have existed as long as there was language or cave drawings to express them.) One of the exciting aspects of this contemporary research is how many knowledge fields are being brought together in intelligent syntheses, such as the integration of physics-neurobiology-mathematical systems.

The events I have already written about—and those that are recorded later in this book—may appear quite extraordinary to you, as they have often been to me. Since they do fall outside the boundaries of our daily conventions, they are indeed extra-ordinary. However, these happenings, vividly true to me, are also linked to thousands of years of similar authentic and recorded mystical experiences. They may be happening to you, too.

Rethinking the Possible

Although I am not a scientist or mathematician, I am using this chapter to suggest how new discoveries in many fields are catalysts for rethinking the meanings of dimensional realities. What are we beginning to understand about new possibilities for viewing our world in different ways and for thinking about the paranormal? Because humans have encountered these experiences "forever," because the outlines of recorded esoteric realities have similar characteristics, and since they often are so profound that our lives and beliefs are turned inside out, many of us are seeking intellectual affirmation by turning to what contemporary science can teach us about complex perceptions. As one researcher and author described it:

> ... in the course of my work, I kept bumping up against miracles. Not miracles in the ordinary sense of the term, where the seas part ... but miracles nonetheless, in their utter violation of the way we think the world works.

These are the observations of Lynne McTaggart, one of the foremost contemporary writers about consciousness, and author of *The Field*. Revisiting scientific discoveries as early as the 1970s and 1980s, she goes on to comment:

> *New discoveries about the mutable nature of atoms and molecules lend more weight to the idea, advanced by a number of these scientists, that consciousness may be central in shaping our world. Dozens of scientists in prestigious areas around the world have demonstrated that all matter exists in a vast quantum web of connection and that an information transfer is constantly going on between living things and their environment. . . . that directed thoughts have a central participatory role in creating reality. . . . The Zero Point Field as a field of all possibility and a free source of unimaginable energy has gripped the public imagination.*

The Zero Point Field, which I will also refer to elsewhere in this narrative, is the point (Zero) at which energy is completely diminished, and yet the possibility of all Energy also exists there. As McTaggart points out, on this scientific frontier researchers have demonstrated that everything is connected, and, "We are an energetic charge. Human beings and all living things are a coalescence of energy connected to every other thing in the world." As this explanation by McTaggart asserts, mystical experiences exist within.

Throughout this narrative, I will often speak of the "Boom!" spiritual experience not only as an epiphany, but as a psychic state marked by Annihilation of the Ego. Since quantum physics reveals that all energy is interconnected, even designations of the "me" and "not-me" are obsolete. Consequently, the previously normative paradigms of our lives must be rethought and redesigned. If our universe is an interconnected, interdependent unity where everything touches everything else at the quantum level, then unquestionably all that exists is one vast energy Field out of which anything may be created by human intent or consciousness. In this world, McTaggart reminds us (quoting Einstein), "The Field is the only reality."

Consider the following scientific insights that have emerged in the past century to demonstrate reality (and metaphysical) paradigms that shift our thinking processes, deepen our comprehension that "all power is in the present moment," and place us in the center of a radiating Field of All Possibilities, out of which substance can be created by our consciousness. The following summary is simplistic but is intended to present these concepts clearly within this narrative framework:

- Time and space as linear and local are obsolete concepts. Everything is relative to the observer, and it may be true that all things "exist" only in the present moment.
- Solid matter does not exist as an impenetrable mass.
- Instead, the universe is a sea of moving, vibrating energy, within which even certain of the smallest subatomic particles may be one thing or another at different times, and may even be many possible things at the same time; they may also die into something else altogether.
- The Field of Energy—of minute particles creating, disappearing, recreating—is, to cite Einstein's words again, "the only reality."
- *Everything*, therefore, is part of this Unified Field.
- We consist only of universal energy (rebonded by universal matter).
- Our thoughts are the energy of the Universal Mind, the timeless web of Intelligence surrounding us.
- Subatomic particles are influenced by our observations.
- Our conscious minds may create or manifest our thoughts in substance.
- "There is no objective world independent of the observer" (as Deepak Chopra suggests).
- At the quantum level, and given that everything vibrates in motion, all things are interdependent and interconnected in a vast, dynamic web; nothing has independent existence.

- A total void or empty space cannot exist; even at Zero Point Field (which marks the closest possibility of total inaction), there is a residue of energy and dynamic activity, out of which new Possibilities can be created.
- Because electrons refuel by tapping into this fluctuating energy of "empty space," the stability of the universe is maintained.

Certainly in this framework, All Possibility exists at the quantum level, and our minds/thoughts can affect the existence of all things. Even more to the point for this narrative, mystical, extra-dimensional experiences are to be expected. Anything may exist, or be created, by our thoughts impacting energy particles.

Although such thoughts may be revolutionary for our world, many ancient philosophers understood these concepts eons ago. We can recall the well-known statement of Asclepius (the Greek healer and founder of medicine): "As above, so below." An ancient adage from India, quoted by Deepak Chopra, recapitulates the concept this way:

> As is the microcosm, so is the macrocosm.
>
> As is the atom, so is the universe.
>
> As is the human body, so is the cosmic body.
>
> As is the human mind, so is the cosmic mind.

Knowing and Becoming

Let me reiterate a basic theorem of the New Physics: Because our new consciousness is defined by the movement and vibration of subatomic particles, out of this vibrating ocean of energy, our thoughts (our attention on the particles) can raise enough energetic power to manifest elements we can intentionally *think* into existence. In this reality, each of us is truly a God particle, as well as a creator of realities. Isn't this mind-blowing?

These concepts are also reminders that we possess multiple ways of Knowing—all of them influenced by culture, myth, history, gender, genetics, etc. This multifaceted approach to understanding knowledge or information can be called a Culture of Inquiry, Questioning, and/ or Critical Thinking. Applied to the search for knowledge in general, it is especially effective in pursuing elusive or complex subjects (the metaphysical, for example), since it engages us in far-ranging questioning of all ideas and experiences from numerous aspects. In this context, possible interpretations of reality push the boundaries of thought until paradigms begin to shift. Additionally, in this methodology, science and the paranormal are not conflicting fields, but can be combined to create new thinking about what *is*. Whether we want to change our reality concepts or not, these ideas are nevertheless transforming everything around us.

Is it so strange, after all, that an aspect of the universe's continuous information transfer is an Intelligent Presence's communication with us? Surely explorations of the metaphysical are a necessary and related element of the Culture of Inquiry. To the mindset of curiosity that desires to embrace everything knowable, we can now add our curiosity about the unknowable, the ineffable esoteric realms. As the psychologist William James asserted in his renowned writing on *The Varieties of Mystical Experience,* "Mysticism is a subject worthy of scientific inquiry." His research on the subject is central to contemporary psychology and will be discussed at greater length in Chapter Five.

Let's also briefly consider the discoveries in brain research that parallel those in quantum physics. Scientists are investigating the phenomenon of brain plasticity, a malleability that allows this organ to retrain itself, actually restructure itself, and transfer functions from one part of the brain to another. A quotation from *The Brain That Changes Itself* by Norman Doidge describes some of these possibilities:

In the course of my travels, I met a scientist who enables people who had been blind since birth to begin to see, another who

*enabled the deaf to hear; I spoke with people who had strokes
decades before, and had been declared incurable, who were
helped to recover with neuroplastic treatments; I met people
whose learning disorders were cured and whose IQs were
raised; I saw evidence that it is possible for eighty year olds
to sharpen their memories to function the way they did when
they were fifty-five. I saw people rewire their brains with their
thoughts, to cure previously incurable obsessions and traumas.
I spoke with Nobel Laureates who were hotly debating how
we must rethink our model of the brain now that we know it
is ever changing.*

As we can perceive in Doidge's observations, the revolution in brain
science, similar to other areas of science, is abundant with transformative potential.

Virtual reality, for example—a phrase so recent that it is not even
in the 2005 dictionary on my desk—is now popularly understood;
some of us may already have experienced these new technologies.
Basically, this is computer-simulated life, complete with replicated
sensory experiences through technological devices such as goggles.
(The rapid advances in this technology may have changed the delivery
system by the time you read this passage.) Influencing human behavior,
adapting cultural norms, and redefining what is real are among anticipated outcomes of this scientific experimentation. Some researchers
even believe they are close to developing tests for reading our thoughts
and our tendencies. Perhaps more important to paranormal study is
the supposition that a sphere of metaphysical energy (think of the
Unified Field) surrounds our physical world. The Unified Field, which
unifies all fundamental forces and elementary particles, is the source
of all consciousness and creation (as well as all aspects of Universal
Intelligence). Although the theory is still debated among scientists, it
nevertheless influences modern scientific thought. Clearly, the intricate
ethical implications inherent in the study of energy fields, including
the integration of reality/virtual reality in our lives, are significant and
are only beginning to be defined.

Brain vs. Mind

At this point, it is helpful to differentiate between the brain and the mind. The brain is the physical organ with its neurological wiring and its capacity to change or renew itself. The mind, on the other hand, is our capacity for consciousness. All the new scientific discoveries are, ultimately, about transformations of consciousness—where expansion of consciousness is at the present moment, and what its future potential might be. Studies of cognitive response at both the conscious and unconscious levels are leading to wider perceptions of how we distinguish what elements impact on human behavior—and how the processes work in our brains and in our minds. Even when mind and body are out of sync, they remain tethered in the ultimate complementarity of mind-brain-body-emotions-spirit. That is, the dislocation of body from mind caused by severe stress (death of a loved one, loss of an important job, bankruptcy) can have devastating effects on the immune system, as the AIDS epidemic demonstrated. However, researchers have also shown that even small stresses—studying for an exam, for example—"adversely affects a very wide range of immunological functions," as a study published by the Fetzer Institute points out and as significant ongoing scientific research indicates. Recent emphases upon prevention of, or amelioration of, disease include increased focus in our culture upon nutrition, exercise, life management and balance, meditation, awareness of genetic markers, recognizing early signs of sickness (such as "Gut Feelings: Stress and the GI Tract"), and so on. These efforts are attempts to restore and/or maintain the vital connections among mind-body-emotions-spirituality.

Obviously, scientists are raising more questions—and more complex ones—about the nature of reality, as well as how brain vs. mind functions, to distinguish various kinds of cognition. At the center of these queries remains the Big Question that affects every field of knowledge: Are we predetermined, or does free will exist? As scientists tap into greater knowledge, they are also able to synthesize more knowledge. Ergo, the more we know, the more we are capable of knowing. At the same time, scholars also uncover more nuanced and variable questions about the conditions of our existence, the circumstances shaping every choice we think we make, and the infinite mysteries of universal intelligence. Each of these elements influences our capacity for awareness of paranormal experiences. Although it may be a stretch of our imagination, the possibility exists that we are programmed to perceive metaphysical experiences. Divine forms, ineffable as they are, still challenge us to know them in this contemporary age and time.

One of the defining works on the subject of the New Science is Fr. Diarmuid O'Murchu's *Quantum Theology: Spiritual Implications of the New Physics*. Essentially, his premise is that the ancient patriarchal church and Divinity do not fit with this time of The Great Shift in technological and scientific thinking. Revolutionary paradigm changes in every knowledge field suggest to Fr. O'Murchu that the intellectual concepts of the church about Divine Energy as disembodied, existing in our heads rather than in our feelings, are archaic. He encourages a personal and emotional fusion with Presence in which we *live* our passion for the Beloved and *feel* the Divine within us. He also reminds us that the interdependence of all things should inspire our commitment to dealing with the Crisis of Ecology, as well as other global crises, understanding that we are linked inextricably to the larger mysteries of the cosmos. Such thinking invites our receptivity to the Divinity that is everywhere, including within each of us.

Neurotheology, as already mentioned, is another significant, emerging field of inquiry. Andrew Newberg, MD, the author of *Principles of Neurotheology*, laid the foundation for the study of how the brain physically changes during religious and ecstatic experiences. Using brain scans to work with nuns, monks, and ordinary people in states of prayer or meditation, he charted changes in brain activity and chemistry during these practices. Not to oversimplify his findings, I can summarize his assertion that the brain is affected by such religious activity, and that, in turn, those changes in the brain affect the nature or intensity of these human experiences. As I write these words, I am once again struck by the interconnectedness of all things.

Dr. Newberg's observations also appear to validate the importance of regular spiritual practices, as well as the power of those practices to create reinforcing patterns in the brain. Given the plasticity of the brain, we could, therefore, deepen the consistency and quality of our religious experiences, including the mystical. Such events could validate the connection between the ethereal and physical reality merging in neuro Possibility. To restate this concept: that which can be imagined can become real—the metaphysical and physical collaborating in active creation.

Throughout this narrative, I make little distinction between religious experiences (which are often doctrinally related, such as the stigmata appearing on the palms of human hands as a mark of purest holiness), and mystical experiences. The characteristics of each often merge: transcendence, appearances by Divine Beings, Annihilation of the Ego, merging into the Deity, and similar occurrences. It is not insignificant that William James, in defining the elements of Mysticism, placed them under the title of *The Varieties of Religious Experience.*

This chapter is intended to raise more questions than can be answered at this point. Although the Science of the Soul points us in the direction of expanded spiritual inquiry, none of these theories prove spiritual Presence in our lives or in the universe. However, we may be edging closer to a time when the Supernatural becomes simply the Natural.

Reflections: Chapter Two

One of the purposes of the Reflections at the end of each chapter is to help you chart your psycho-spiritual changes while reading this book. This is, after all, a narrative that pushes the margins, and your complex reactions are inevitable. You may feel anger, confusion, and uncertainty, along with anticipation, heightened curiosity, and exhilaration.

Acknowledge your responses, whatever they may be. Remember, this narrative is not a "passive read."

We often feel resistance when faced with changes, even those changes we willingly choose to make. At first it might feel unnatural, but, given time, new habits and routines become second nature. The Science of the Soul points to exciting new connections that will have an unavoidable impact on each of our lives.

1. In your current belief system, what do you consider possible, and not possible? Record your thoughts. Then read them aloud to yourself. Do you have different perspectives on what you believe as you hear yourself saying the words?
2. Define any resistance you feel to the New Science and the concepts discussed in this chapter. Are you angry, dismissive, unsettled, curious, excited? What other feelings emerge as you think about this chapter? If, on the other hand, you are not resistant but receptive, define those feelings instead.
3. Now consider Lynne McTaggart's description of "the field of all possibility and a free source of unimaginable energy." She is informing us that this infinite creative energy is universally accessible. How does that possibility affect you, and in what specific ways?
4. What salient events have you experienced that might affirm the existence of this "field of all possibility"?

CHAPTER THREE

Mystical Foremothers

My Swedish grandmother conjured me.

That statement may appear dramatic and surprising. But it is also true. By *conjuring*, I mean "to bring something about by invocation, rite, and ritual." Although conjuring may be used for good or ill, her intention was to call forth an act of grace. Grandmother Hannah, performing her Eastern Star rituals in 1938, did not perceive them as bizarre, witchy, or dark. On the contrary, her words were an invocation to evoke the birth of her granddaughter. This conjuring, which took place on the eve of WWII, is more readily understood within the cultural and historical context of that time.

Because we live now in the daily reality of continuous warfare and atrocity somewhere or other around the globe, that is our Normal. So it may be difficult to imagine a time in which war was seen as an end game. As historians look back at events, World War II—abhorrent and genocidal as it was—was viewed by both the Allies (the United States, Great Britain and cohorts) and the Axis (Germany, Italy, Japan and cohorts) as the one final war to be reluctantly undertaken as an epic struggle between Good and Evil, Light and Darkness, the War to End All Wars. For both the Allies and the Third Reich (Germany), it was a battle to determine which philosophy of the world would shape the global future.

A prominent Campaign of the Occult (supernatural beliefs, practices, and phenomena employed for propaganda purposes) was waged by both the Allies and the Third Reich before and throughout the war. Each side sought to prove by publicity or propaganda techniques (films, radio talks, and programs, leaflets dropped by air, as well as more subtle

29

methods) that they were the faction favored by Spirits of Light, those supernatural forces that guided military decisions, protected military forces, and provided paranormal answers to the outcomes of battles and the fate of the world. Desperate times—and WWII was surely a desperate time—have often called for a cultural suspension of disbelief allowing for supernatural forces to be called upon to achieve real and metaphorical victory (Joshua at the Battle of Jericho, and the exploits of the warrior David are well-known examples).

Grandmother Hannah, like so many other American citizens, became part of the extended effort to oppose the rising darkness of the Axis countries. Just as Grandfather was a Freemason, so she became a high priestess in Eastern Star, committing herself to Holding the Light. Nightly, before my conception (as my aunt later told me), my grandmother strode back and forth across the living room, a book of mystic rituals open in her hand, chanting the words that she believed would call forth the Light Spirit of her granddaughter. I was to be that granddaughter.

You may wonder at this point: What do the tales I'm about to tell about my Mystical Foremothers (grandmothers and mother) have to do with you? I use their stories as illustrations of my family's paranormal history to inspire and encourage you to think of your own family accounts of strange happenings. Most of us have such tales in our backgrounds. Whether the events were recounted dismissively by the teller or narrated as ancestral mysteries, they impacted your sense of reality. I invite you to recall and seek out, if you are able, the experiences of your own Mystical Foremothers and Forefathers. Knowledge of your personal history can create for you a more intimate connection to other realities. In my case, this background prepared me for events to come in my life, including the dimensional shift at Karnak.

Breaking Barriers of Perception

When I was born on Easter Sunday, a blessed Festival of Light in both Christian and pagan mythology (I use *pagan* as a neutral word to mean simply non-Judeo-Christian religions), Grandmother Hannah perceived this birth timing as a Divine sign of answered prayers. From the moment I drew breath, she and I possessed a mystical connection. Obviously, her interest in the paranormal was a significant force in my life. So, too, were the beliefs of my mother, Helen. Sharing some of the stories they told me may prime the pump of your imagination and are integral to the context of this book. They shaped how I perceived the world, and suggested the existence of possibilities that lie beyond our ken. Each one had separately lived supernatural experiences that they did not dismiss out of hand. I would say now they unwittingly created portals in my mind. Later, it was my choice to open those portals.

There is a perfect quote from Rosamund Stone Zander about the realities of our lives and how we comprehend them. In *The Art of Possibility*, she says, "We *perceive* only the sensations we are programmed to receive, and our awareness is further restricted by the fact that we *recognize* only those for which we have mental maps or categories." That philosophical framework, combined with Hannah's and Helen's mystical bent, enriches the substance of my narrative.

In this regard, Zander's writing further enlarged my metaphysical understanding. She cites a splendid quote from neurophysiologist Donald O. Hebb: "The 'real world' is a construct. . . ." Zander goes on to remind us of what Albert Einstein told Heisenberg (contemporary mathematical physicist and Einstein's colleague) in 1926: that it made no sense to develop theories based only on observable facts. "In reality," Einstein explained, "the very opposite happens. It is theory which decides what we can observe." Zander emphasizes the point by the title of the initial chapter of her book: "It's All Invented." Most of us are familiar with the common phrase, "Our minds create our own realities," a concept adjacent to the use of visualization to create anything we can imagine. The thought is infinitely empowering.

Yet a puzzling paradox exists in our culture. We are suspicious of esoteric occurrences, but some of the most popular television series for the past fifty years are *Bewitched* (witches, warlocks, and magic made homey), *I Dream of Jeannie* (the ancient Arabian tale of the genie in the bottle brought up-to-date), *Supernatural* (ghosts, demons, angels, and every supernatural permutation possible), *Charmed* (a charming trio of witches), and more recently, *Sleepy Hollow* (a stew of everything supernatural), and *Proof* (near-death experiences). I have not even mentioned the many TV series about living vampires and werewolves. Traditionally, we tell ghost stories around campfires to youthful enthusiasts, enticing their imaginations, as well, perhaps as their belief in mystical events. Within our cultural framework, however, we do not usually intend for them to actually buy into the tales. In the cold light of day, we remain skeptical about these realities. We invent the stories, or we recreate them from the past, but we often don't actually believe them.

It is not surprising, then, that the repetitious question that is usually raised about accounts of mystical experiences—"Is it true?"—is really a question springing out of doubt, as well as our limited perceptions and assumptions surrounding the events. Or, as we commonly put it today, "Our minds create our realities." To that end, let me share more about the ways in which Hannah and Helen provided the varied pieces for the mosaic of my worldview, as your ancestors' recollections most likely created yours.

My Great-grandmother, Eva, was also one of my Mystical Foremothers. She carried the heritage of generations of Swedish female healers and midwives with her, those women who practiced knowledge they would never call "occult," but which was nevertheless infused with faith in miraculous healing rituals, the power of incantations, and prayers answered from whatever source. Following old traditions (some of it learned from the forest and mountain "witches"), they blended ancient use of plants and herbs with spells and Christian prayers. The dark and moody Scandinavian landscape and climate may well have provoked a need to befriend any and all powers of Light.

Occult Scandinavian myths seeped into my blood and bones as I listened to Hannah's tales of healing, magic powers, and casting of the runes. These were as much a part of my childhood as were the Biblical stories of Noah and the Flood, Abraham and Sarah, Ruth and Naomi—realities that coexisted and intertwined with elements of the

Mysteries. As already suggested, you most likely have similar knowledge in your backgrounds, the recall of which empowers your own mystical memories. Although Grandmother sometimes dismissed her tales with the comment, "Oh, well, it's just superstition" (and she would chuckle and tap me on the knee to indicate the story was told all in good fun), she also described some of her own supernatural experiences more matter-of-factly. I recall how she and her immigrant family had settled in northern Michigan, where winters were long, cold, and hard, not unlike the Sweden they had left. In this setting, sounds without a source and people who seemingly appeared and suddenly disappeared were not uncommon.

One Sunday, as Hannah told this particular tale, her entire family heard sleigh bells, along with the laughter of adults and children, coming down the snowy road; in still, clear air, sound carries a far distance. Expecting visitors, Eva and the children hurried to set the table and set out food as coffee perked, while Great-grandfather cleared the front path. The sleigh bells, talking voices, and snorting horses came almost up to the house—and then abruptly ceased. When Hannah's family walked outside, no one was there, and there were no fresh tracks in the snow. It was a mystery, one among many Hannah encountered as she was growing up.

My mother (who represented the other side of my family) also carried a lineage of spirit visits and other psychic phenomenon. Her father, who died of cancer when she was twelve, lived his last few months in wretched pain. Each night after he came home from work and pulled his cancer-wracked body up the stairs, she was awakened by his moans. For months after his death, the nightly sounds continued. The family was further haunted within a year by the deaths of Helen's beloved grandmother and the drowning of her older sister on high school graduation day. Following these traumas, my mother was at once comforted and made uneasy by the appearance of a silent nun who rocked in the chair beside her bed each night.

Tales such as these were unforgettable. The little girl (me) who listened to them took it all in; she had already had the first of her own mystical experiences.

33

Wolf at the Door

That mystical event happened when I was about two years old and already possessed a prodigious vocabulary. I knew how to express myself.

In an indelible memory, I recall standing up in my crib, holding onto the wooden guard bars, as I heard knocking on the apartment door. When the door swung open by itself, a huge wolf entered. He padded to my crib, rose up on his hind legs, and silently gazed at me. His was an overpowering presence, as spiritual manifestations often are. I remember wanting to call out, but my voice was frozen.

Years later, I still remember every detail: the animal's immense and burning eyes; the thick gray-black fur that made him appear even larger; and a great head that loomed over me. Most of all, I felt wrapped in an energy I cannot accurately describe even now. As soon as my throat opened up, I screamed for my mother, and the canine figure evaporated. As I grew into adolescence, I often recalled this dream, so powerful was the image and my accompanying emotions. Years later, I finally asked my mother about the experience. She affirmed how frightened I had been by the appearance of the Great Wolf and how I had struggled to describe it. I had insisted the wolf was real, she told me. Then she would add ruefully, "Daddy was on the GI Bill—and we were so poor that the wolf was always at our door."

Yet I never doubted that the wolf actually stood by my crib. If I relax, close my eyes, and concentrate, I can still feel his breath on my face and his rough coat brushing my arm. The *why* of the dream remained hidden until I began serious metaphysical study at mid-life. By then, the childhood experience had receded into my unconscious. Still, when the spiritual teacher led me in an exercise to discover my totem, the animal that revealed itself was—of course—a wolf. Only then did I remember the Great Wolf's appearance many years before.

That early reality/dreamlike experience ushered in a lifetime of mystical experiences. Many spiritual presences appeared to me as time passed. The figure of Hecate (Goddess of Transformation), for example, ushered in six weeks of episodic dreaming during a period of major life changes; She foreshadowed the lengthy Dreaming Time to come with the Divine Being, Sekhmet, as I narrate later. The Egyptian Goddess Isis also visited me twice at night during difficult times, bringing Her nurturing energy and the message, "All is well." This phrase, as I and others have found, is a reassurance often given during visits by Spirit Guides, Angels, and other Divine Forces. Each messenger always concludes an appearance with these words: "All is well." As you will understand in ensuing chapters, it is the eternal promise Sekhmet gives after every communication.

This chapter has travelled quite a distance from Grandmother Hannah conjuring me, to the uses of the occult by both warring sides during WWII, to supernormal events within my family, to my own mystical experiences. I have provided this global and personal background to demonstrate the sweep of supernatural influences on the world stage, as well as in my private experiences. The paranormal has existed from the beginning of language and cave art (at least as expressions of human perceptions), suggesting that some kind of God-Force or Universal Intelligence may have been, or believed to have been, present. Whether we acknowledge it or not, mysticism and the supernatural permeate our myths and our history. My story is part of that web of myth, dreams, Divine Presence, and mystery—as is yours.

You may wonder how I have remembered so many details of the experiences I share with you. Even as a child, I wrote down important events, conversations and descriptions as a means of imbedding them also in my memory. Since being a writer was my life's goal, I understood the necessity of training the memory, as well as of keeping a record of my experiences and thoughts. Although many of those diaries are now gone, my memories remain vivid. In addition, every syllable of the dream narrative is based on my extensive written journals and recollections, as I recount later. I hope this book presents new, and challenges old, assumptions for you. Your own encounters with Spirit, of course, cannot exactly replicate my experiences, but my accounts may trigger some of your forgotten memories. However this narrative may serve you, I acknowledge that each one of us is faced only with the revelations allowed by our own spiritual templates.

Reflections: Chapter Three

To paraphrase my comments at the conclusion of Chapter One, the following reflective questions concluding each chapter encourage you to personalize this information to your life and experiences. Use the queries to delve deeper into the ideas presented and test their authenticity against your own thoughts and experiences.

1. As you think about your family lore and traditions, what remarkable or strange experiences come to mind?
2. When Rosamund Stone Zander states, "We *perceive* only the sensations we are programmed to receive. . . . We *recognize* only those for which we have mental maps or categories," what does that mean to you and your life?
3. This quotation presents us with a less-structured perception of reality. What core beliefs (list four of them) currently shape your sense of reality?
4. As you are thinking about these ideas, what evolving beliefs or paradigms might modify or even replace some of your current ones?
5. How do you *feel* as you address question #4 (e.g., anticipatory, fearful, angry, joyful)? Do you understand why these are your reactions? Will these reactions help or hinder you in considering different thought paradigms as you continue reading this narrative?

CHAPTER FOUR

Show Me How to Do This

Let's begin this chapter where my own paranormal experiences temporarily concluded—with total surrender to the power of the Sacred. Rather than merely defining the words *mystic, mystical,* and *Mysticism,* I have described the feelings of that mystic event so that meaning comes alive through the description. As a reader, you can comprehend the awe evoked my submitting to Sekhmet's claim. The experience is classic in its characteristics: ineffable, all-encompassing, emotionally intense, obliterating time and space, ego annihilating. Her presence illustrates the essence of Mysticism. She *is* the Living Mystery.

Some readers may feel wary about concepts like mystics, mysteries, and Mysticism. These words, however, describe experiences that lift the veil, amplifying our consciousness of the Divine and the Divinity within. Universal Energy, the spiritual force that desires to be known by each of us, can be visualized as a bundle of metaphysical synapses within our spiritual and physical nerve centers. We react to its vibrations with nerves jangling and heightened consciousness. Every sense responds in high alert. We are snapped awake by alignment with a supernatural power that continuously communicates its messages to us, gifting us with mysterious—often opaque—events, dreams, symbols, and images. This is the spiritual "Stuff," the Real Deal, with which we create the stories and myths of our lives. Even when we are too distracted to receive that Divine invitation in the moment, we can trust that it will come again. Remember that the Source does not hide from us; in our vulnerability and ambivalence, we hide from the Source.

Although this may seem like a cosmic game of hide and seek, this is not a game. It is a metaphysical experience, the meaning of which we have to discover for ourselves. Each of us has life purposes, missions, sacred contracts, and quests that lead us to discovery of the Divine self within.

"Don't tell me about it! Show me how to do it myself," is a natural reaction in my seminars. "I don't just want to know what happened to you; I want to know how to make it happen to me."

All right, then. Here is one process that can help you find the pathway into your own mysteries. To follow that path, let's begin with three premises:

- A Divine Presence dwells within each of us;
- Connection with this Divine Energy is not only possible for each individual, but it is the loving and compassionate intent of God-Beings to reveal it to us;
- The spiritual process itself need not be complex, whatever the God-Being Who calls us. Think, for example, of the profound simplicity of the Lord's Prayer or Lincoln's Gettysburg Address. The prayer leads us to our inner Divinity, while the speech called for the healing of a divided nation. Each is remarkable for brevity, clarity, and simplicity.

These premises are a foundation upon which the five steps, outlined below, are constructed. Although the actions are uncomplicated, your effort is still required. Spiritual inquiry is not an enterprise for the dilettante, but one for those who authentically seek to know.

The following five steps are a process (aspects of increased consciousness) designed for easy recall, and each one evolves our spiritual—and self—knowledge. Ideally, these phases are sequential. More likely, however, they will overlap, merge, and sometimes jump out of sequence before they slip back into place. Remember, any process that fosters the growth of consciousness has to be, by its nature, fluid.

Let's look at these five elements of increased consciousness:

Awareness or Awakening
Attention
Accessibility
Assimilation
Action

This process is intentionally brief. Hundreds of books have been written elaborating on each step, and I do not intend to replicate that good work. These are suggestions, reminders of what we each already know, that can catalyze our personal journeys. The points provide a simple scaffolding upon which heightened consciousness can be constructed.

Awareness

Have you sometimes, or often, been so preoccupied with the time compression of daily life that you can't remember at night what you ate for lunch? Or what the weather was like two days ago? We are so busy being busy! Many of us have strolled through our lives like T. S. Eliot's modern "hero," J. Alfred Prufrock. "I have measured out my life," says Prufrock, "with coffee spoons." As we symbolically step into Awareness, we signify a willingness to participate fully in the life we own and to ignite our consciousness. No longer measuring our lives with coffee spoons, we make a choice to awaken to the world and to ourselves. In choosing Becoming over passivity, we initiate our transformation into receptive consciousness—without which enlightenment is not possible.

We are Seekers.

Attention

Awareness naturally morphs into the phase of Attentiveness. Here, our intentional, concentrated focus expands our perceptions to include the Visible and Invisible. We may not comprehend all aspects of the brink we stand on, yet in the Gap between these realms of Visible/ Invisible lies the power of manifestation and spiritual awakening. By acts of Attention and intention (declaring our intentions to the universe is a significant act, inviting the assistance of supernatural powers), we become capable of blurring spiritual, physical, and intellectual boundaries; of drawing nearer, through our unfolding experiences, to closing the Gap and glimpsing the Mysteries. Our worlds will tilt, since discovery is never static. That psychic tilt, however, is a piece of the process of Becoming. Everything is change—so, yes, we are called to pay Attention.

My first spiritual teacher provided my introduction to authentic Attention when she gave me a simple action to perform at the start of my metaphysical training. "Choose a favorite flower," she said. "Spend the next three days, with complete attention, studying it carefully. Come to know every gradation of color and hue at each time of day; learn how the blossom's odors change from morning to noon to evening. Notice how the scent changes from bud, to bloom, to the flower's decay. How does the flower respond to your presence? To the sound of your voice?" She continued with other questions as she trained me to *see* the world: to pay Attention.

This exercise, along with others, did teach me about Attentiveness, not merely to the flower, but to the larger world, to see beyond surface impressions. That teacher-mentor taught me a practice of sense-attention to decode my visions and dreams in Egypt and afterwards. In time, using practices like these, each of us can develop a habit of attentive presence that opens deeper knowing (the fabled Third Eye).

Let's push the margins of Attention even farther. The more adept we become in projecting Attention as a mental and energetic force, the more effectively we can use the tools of visualization. To demonstrate, let's take our minds off the leash and play with such disparate elements as manifestation, the Gap, mind power, and Olympic athletics to illustrate a metaphysical process. The most effective training techniques used for Olympic athletes—combining guided visualizations with sports practice sessions—are well known and well replicated.

Trainers, coaches, researchers, and athletes have proven that what the mind can visualize, it can create. Most of you are already familiar with the idea, since a popular movie used the same concepts to invent *A Field of Dreams.*

Perhaps we can understand visualizing or imagining outcomes as a kind of preview of the Mysteries (it is also, of course, a study in brain science), since the action goals are manifestations created by our mind power. It is said of Michelangelo, for example, that before he set chisel to marble, he already saw the fully conceived statue in the stone. His artistic job, then, was to manifest what he saw in his vision. Later in this narrative, I will tell the fabulous story of Montserrat College, a dying art school which was recreated through the power of visualization translated into action.

In a similar way, this book was conceived in my mind and developed through mental imagery (even to the color of the cover page). It has now become a reality because years ago I could see it, hear the words in my head, relive the mystic events through visualization, viscerally remember the energy surrounding those events, and feel the physical sensation of holding the book. Now, as I actually experience the weight of that book in my hands, I know that *Fire in the Soul* existed as a metaphysical reality waiting to be manifest long before I sat down at the computer to write.

Accessibility

Each of us possess our own gifts and sensitivities in our approach to experiencing realities, as well as to interpreting them. Our own innate spiritual capacities are astonishing. Every spiritual insight that comes to us emanates from a Source which draws upon our Awareness and Attention. In this continuous loop of energy, the Impossible *is* Possible, as I repeat often in this narrative. What I have done and experienced, I share with you as an illustration of what each of you also can do.

Spiritual Accessibility, however, is a two-way street: just as we seek access to spiritual Mysteries, Divine Being seeks Accessibility to us. Our real spiritual journey is the inner one, the quest for knowledge of the Divinity within. This may indeed be why we simultaneously yearn for, and fear, this journey. We intuitively know that before it ends, we will have braved our darkest shadows, leaped into the Deep, dropped our masks to reveal the vulnerable Self stripped of Ego, and been reborn.

Inevitably, our inner journeys mirror our quests in the external world. The fire in our souls drives some of us to trek across the Himalayas, teach in a school for the blind in India, set up a studio for itinerant artists in rural Italy, build schools in Iraq, fly helicopters in Afghanistan, or plunge into other transformative experiences. *Wild,* the life-changing journey of Cheryl Strayed, *had* to find its own shape; it morphed into an arduous physical quest that revealed her ardent spirit and God-Soul. Vicariously through media and books, we have witnessed the unique and individualized journey of Stephen Hawking that has taken place primarily in his wheelchair, with telescopes, Internet, books, and his vast mind as resources. Inner and outer quests come together ironically in Hawking's life: wheelchair-bound, yet unrestricted in the flights of his curious mind. Whatever the outer conditions of our lives, spiritual possibilities are infinitely accessible to our consciousness.

Although I have already described the meaning of my journey to Egypt, let me restate that it occurred because a particular Divine Energy spun me around and called me there. My outer quest served the inner purposes of my evolving consciousness. Although spiritual Mysteries are complex, the ineluctable starting point of our spiritual process is wherever we are in the Now. The simplicity of that statement is profound. At any moment, at any place or time, we can enter the Unknown. As Sekhmet urges us, "Pay attention!"

Assimilation

Fragmentary knowledge is of limited use to those of us who seek. Only through the process of assimilating and integrating those fragments are we granted an amplified power of Knowing. At this point, we understand the Possible as the existence of, and Accessibility to, the Source: Sacred

Unity, Balance, Perfect Order, and Equilibrium. This is the Still Point of all Being. It is the moment of total surrender. It is the gap between the breaths. When we no longer feel the need to defend and protect our "I" identity, then we gain the freedom to detach from the world's contradictions. In detachment, a holy equilibrium of consciousness is possible, a condition where light and dark are harmonized within us, and inner chaos is replaced with Divine order.

Action

In all things spiritual, as already stated, it is not enough to know. Spirituality is not passive state; it is creative, transforming, loving, and sometimes fiery. Each of us who seek the Source will—through our choices—breathe life into knowledge, and compassion into our actions. Johann Wolfgang von Goethe, the nineteenth century German poet and philosopher, eloquently affirms the requirement of spiritual action in his familiar lines, "Knowing is not enough; we must apply. Willing is not enough; we must do." Similarly, other philosophers, theologians, and writers for centuries have shared their belief that wisdom and knowledge are imbued with an obligation to affect the outer world through our actions.

If you don't know where to start—and often we do not—remember the words of Thomas Carlyle, nineteenth-century philosopher, author, and social reformer: "Do the work that lies nearest thee." Or, as Pema Chodron (American Buddhist nun and author) says, "Start where you are." Whatever action is near at hand (accessible) is the fountainhead of spiritual action. Each of us knows intuitively what challenges call to us. We don't need tarot cards, incense, or colored candles to tell us what to do. As in many metaphysical things, *Keep it simple* is the best principle to follow.

Another quotation from Goethe reminds us that our evolving consciousness empowers us to bring knowing and action into balance. Acknowledging how challenging it is—even with the best metaphysical tools at hand—to practice what we know, Goethe said, "Thinking is easy, acting is difficult, and to put one's thoughts into action is the most difficult thing in the world."

Reflections: Chapter Four

Since each of us wants to know how to connect with the Mysteries (there are no absolute formulas), this chapter suggests five practices to assist us: Awareness, Attention, Accessibility, Assimilation, and Action.

1. Are any of these five practices especially effective for you? Which ones speak to you, and why are those more resonant for you?
2. Metaphysical researchers commonly assert that the stronger the emotions in the imaging (feelings being forms of energy), the more quickly reality manifests. How does this idea fit with your own experiences of visualization?
3. Throughout the narrative, we have been discussing—and will continue to discuss—the importance of envisioning the Possible. Is your perception of the Possible changing by this point in the narrative? What does it mean to you now?
4. Why did I ask you question #3?

CHAPTER FIVE

Mystery of Mysteries

William James—often called the Father of American Psychology, author, Harvard professor, and researcher—was one of the most productive and respected minds of the late nineteenth and earlier twentieth centuries. He perceived, and helped define, the common threads emerging in the fields of psychology, theology, philosophy, and American culture, among other elements. As his scholarly observations crossed the boundaries of academic fields, he also honed his intellectual curiosity.

Why does his curiosity matter in this narration? Because of it, his mind was open to an array of intellectual and human possibilities, including paranormal events. After James had encountered his own mystical experiences, he laid the foundation for scientific interest in this phenomenon. His encouragement of colleagues to take the subject of psychic research seriously as a worthy field for study marked a change in academic attitudes toward the supernatural. This was not a sea change, however, given the skepticism of many scholars, a skepticism which still continues today. But it was an open declaration by an established academic voice that mystical events were real, that there were defining characteristics for them, and that he was giving legitimacy to paranormal research. By addressing the value of this topic as a scholarly undertaking, he brought the study of metaphysics out of the academic shadows.

Because James's descriptions of the esoteric are still accurate, because he presents them so cogently, and because he believed mystical experiences could be an aspect of psycho-spiritual human experience, the following summary of his ideas adds validation to this narrative. James was of the opinion, as am I, that these esoteric occurrences were accessible to most of us, as he writes in *Varieties of Religious Experience*:

> *Our normal waking consciousness, rational consciousness as we call it, is but one special type of consciousness, whilst all about it, parted from it by the filmiest of screens, there lie potential forms of consciousness entirely different. We may go through life without suspecting their existence; but apply the requisite stimulus, and at a touch they are there in all their completeness . . .*

Acknowledging obliviousness as a common state of mind, he suggests that a triggering event or stimulus has the power to expose a different consciousness. Moreover, he states, that event will not be fragmentary, but will appear as a full-blown experience.

In this remarkable passage, he also affirms the ancient concept of the "the veil" as "the filmiest of screens" separating rational from mystical consciousness. "Lifting the veil" that metaphorically hides esoteric mysteries is a revelatory act that holds out the potential of exposing supernatural secrets. In addition, James's well-known phrase, "mystical states of consciousness," casts a wide net to encompass events from the non-religious to the intensely religious. Clarifying the broad sweep of mystical possibilities, in both *Varieties* and "A Suggestion about Mysticism," he designates four characteristics all these events have in common:

- These experiences are noetic: of the mind or intellect, over and beyond their emotional impact. As James states, "Although similar to states of feeling, mystical states seem to those who experience them to be also states of knowledge."
- They are ineffable—outside the boundaries of rational explanation; not only do we have no context within which to describe them, but we possess no language exquisite enough to describe "the levels of full-body sensation."
- The experiences are transient, in the sense that they fade away quickly and are difficult to recall with precision. (How right

46

was my mentor, Bob Masters, to insist, as I point out later, that my dream experiences be recorded immediately upon waking, before everyday life could blur the edges of my memory!)

- They are passive experiences; that is, we cannot process the significance of the experience as it is occurring; the events "seem to happen without *our* will" or intention, as Sandra Stahlman says in her web commentary on James (Institute of Peak States website).

Stahlman further explains that, in these "passive experiences," the boundaries of the ego become less distinct, while at the same time the Self expands. I would describe this even more graphically: we merge into a universal body of energy. As that happens, our potential receptivity to the paranormal expands, allowing mystical experiences to occur more frequently thereafter. It makes sense that once the gates of awareness are opened, metaphysical experiences can recur.

My experiences with Sekhmet illustrate James's observations. When the Goddess appeared at Karnak, and later when I surrendered to Her at last, a sacred portal opened within me. She granted me a receptive consciousness that would bear witness to another Mystery: nearly a year of Her continuous dream narratives (which I describe in Chapters 10 through 13).

Defining the Authentic Mystical Event

My own definition of Mysticism is this: "a transfigurative and mysterious event, centered on an intense, all-consuming paranormal experience with a Divine Presence, beyond the limits of rational understanding."

To James's characteristics of an authentic mystical experience (noetic, ineffable, transient, passive), I am appending five additional characteristics. These five consistent markers reflect my observations of these events. They are present, additionally, in Biblical visitations, spiritual memoirs, and paranormal depictions found in a variety of sacred materials, as well as in the accounts of individuals who have been in my seminars and/or been interviewed by me. Additionally, a contemporary body of written accounts (such as Eben Alexander's *Proof of Heaven*) now exists to amplify our understanding of the phenomena. I only wish I had possessed this knowledge before Karnak; it would have prepared me for the tumultuous sensations of that encounter.

These are my additions to James's descriptions.

1. **Transcendence of Time and Space.** When a mystical event seizes us, we are suddenly nowhere and yet everywhere, as the physical world falls away. The veil between dimensions lifts. In that moment, there is no time or space; we are thrust into Infinity. At Karnak, the walls dissolved and the ground disappeared underfoot as I was transported by Sekhmet onto an etheric plane. James refers to this phenomenon as a *noetic* experience ("of the mind and the intellect"), a point essential enough to be reemphasized. An experience of the Mysteries is more than an emotional encounter.

2. **The Experience of Unconditional Love and Compassion.** Unlike any other experiences in our lives, this is "being in the Presence of the Living God." We are baptized in an ocean of rapture and a new experience of faith (whatever form that belief takes). The radiance of Sekhmet's countenance as she extended her Light, love, and compassion swept away all my other perceptions. She unquestionably embraced my imperfect spirit, ecstatically, without judgment.

3. **Intense Intimacy with the Sacred.** The passion for a God-Being has traditionally been described within institutionalized religion as a Sacred Marriage; Catholic nuns, for example, wear wedding rings as symbols of their marriage in Christ. As I have already said, I fell in love with Sekhmet, who became my spiritual Beloved and Adored One. The sacred intimacy of the experience becomes a fusion with Divine Being. Although it may sound like hyperbole, those who receive a mystical vision invariably describe the feeling evoked as a "rapture." I, too, was lost in rapture with Sekhmet.

4. **Annihilation of the Ego.** As the God/dess revealed Herself, I flowed into Her. "I" no longer existed.

5. **Terror**—or, at the other extreme—**serenity.** Although these contradictory possibilities may seem confusing, remember that mystical occurrences are extraordinary, beyond our rational knowing. Whatever are the sensations we feel, the event is a comprehensive experience, engulfing every aspect of our consciousness. Although the differentiated "I" no longer exists, paradoxically, the Soul-Self energetically expands to become greater than it has ever been.

Biblical and other accounts often cite *trembling* as a typical response (which was one of my reactions at Karnak). Whatever the reaction is, terrible or exultant or serene (and everything in between), its power overwhelms us. One final comment about the reaction of terror is helpful: In *The Teachings of the Mystics,* W. T. Stace has written, "It should be carefully noted that only fully developed mystical experiences are necessarily apprehensive" (that is, our mystical awareness may include anxiety and fear if the event fully embodies the major characteristics outlined by James and other scholars, as well as my descriptions).

Expanding Perceptions

Albert Einstein (almost every researcher's go-to source) captures the essence of the mystical experience in these words:

> *The most beautiful and profound emotion we can experience is the sensation of the mystical. . . . To know what is impenetrable to us really exists, manifesting itself as the highest wisdom and the most radiant beauty.*

"Impenetrable," "highest wisdom," "the most radiant beauty"—these words are apt descriptors. Still, the impenetrability of the manifold mystical experience, including that which remains concealed, is elusive.

One of those elusive elements is the difference between *being* and *becoming*. The Mystery is so profound—imagine being thrust into an infinity without boundaries, beyond time and space, your ego identity absorbed into a Divine Energy too unknowable to name and too powerful to comprehend—that no external markers exist. And what we know internally cannot be explained by words. That is the Mystery.

To encounter this experience is to be gripped and transformed by an accelerated spiritual evolution. From the point of the encounter onward, nothing will be the same. We move from a static condition to becoming a soul in motion. Another way to express the change is to discern it as a movement from metaphysical simplicity to an awakening into metaphysical complexity, where surface reality is merely a veneer over the infinite Unified Field. Drawn into the spiritual dynamism of Becoming, why wouldn't we be open to mystical experiences? As the English philosopher, Alfred North Whitehead, brilliantly stated, "God is self-experiential, in that it is the nature of the Universe to experience itself." It is also the nature of humankind to pursue the meaning of the Divine Enigma, to discover the God-particle within each of us.

At the Gates of Mystical Study

Let's speculate now on the link between Mysticism and the mysterious Mystery Schools, those sites of intellectual-psycho-spiritual learning that hugely expanded knowledge across the ancient world in virtually every field: physics, mathematics, astrology, history, poetry, philosophy, theology, geography, myth, and so on. This section of the narrative is not a careless diversion. Instead, it is an illustration of humankind's ancient longing to explain that which is unknowable by attempting to prove it through that which is already known. These methodologies were also attempts to expand consciousness through completing increasingly difficult intellectual stages which could be attained only through discipline and years of study. In this context, it was theorized, the Mysteries could be unveiled and interpreted. Although most of the specific discoveries of the Mystery Schools have been lost, that intentional seeking for meaning certainly exists to this day.

The lure of hidden or esoteric knowledge goes back to the beginnings of recorded history. Seductive and enticing tales of mysterious and forbidden knowledge permeate all cultures and times. Most of us, for example, recognize the familiar themes of the Garden of Eden story: sacred and concealed knowledge (perhaps the Mysteries themselves), forbidden by the Biblical God, is nevertheless sought by two human beings who are rewarded with the burden of sin in exchange for lost paradise. Thus, as legends tell us, the alluring quest is dangerous and may not end well.

A sidebar observation would now be helpful in this discussion. It is not surprising that secret societies of elite members (those who have undergone rigorous training to decipher sacred knowledge) have emerged, from ancient times to the present: adepts of the Mystery Schools, Knights Templar, the Vatican Curia, the Masonic Order, to cite only a few. As author Jeanne M. House points out, ". . . secret societies throughout time provide the ongoing link to the hidden world." Just as thousands of years ago, Mystery Schools preserved esoteric secrets and then passed them on to worthy initiates through structured studies and experiences, secret societies enlarged the circle of initiates, while still maintaining at least the guise of hidden mysteries.

Returning again to the central topic, I emphasize that the connection between Mysticism and the Mystery Schools is momentous. Because many details of the Schools, as well as the Mysteries themselves, are opaque, and because the purpose of this book is not primarily to focus on the Mystery Schools, my observations will have to be limited. Even so, I will provide enough information to illustrate key concepts and outline major links between the Mysteries, our current revelational times, and my mysterious journey with Sekhmet.

In the ancient world—notably Egypt, Persia, Chaldea, Greece, Rome, the Yucatan Peninsula, India, China—Mystery Schools were well established (the earliest may date back to 3,500 years ago). Although we have no first-person accounts of these Schools, we do have fragmentary historical records of their existence across many cultures. They were psycho-spiritual in nature (the interrelatedness of human behavior/ thought and spirituality) and provided spiritual and intellectual training for priests, Magi, philosophers (such as Plato), mathematicians (Euclid, Pythagoras), healers (Asclepius), and Masters of Wisdom (Socrates, Aristotle), among others. Since each of these names is recorded in the extant manuscript fragments, we can reasonably assume that the Mystery Schools were held in high regard and that they attracted the most gifted students. To the best of our knowledge, the educational process involved symbolic passages or levels, doors or Gates, each of which required successful completion of sacred tasks and, usually, a capstone challenge before admittance to the highest level. Even the years of rigorous study required for each level did not guarantee progress to the next one. Pythagoras, as an illustration, took twenty-two years, and many trials, to achieve the final level.

Although we do not possess certainty about the specifics of each level or the types of required testing of skills and knowledge, some scholars and researchers suggest that nine Gates had to be passed through (some historians theorize six or seven Gates), each one representing an area of expertise. (Egyptian priests went through six levels or Orders, passing through each stage after reading the required number of texts by Hermes: works of magic, alchemy, and astrology—subjects intertwined with mathematics and physics.) It appears feasible that modern quantum physics, neurology, and studies of the brain may have their roots in the concepts and challenges of these Schools. Human fascination with the subject, and the desire to participate in such learning, did not die with the disappearance of ancient civilizations. There are several versions of the Mystery Schools available today; you can find their descriptions on the Internet and conduct your own due diligence about the quality of these programs.

Another observation can be made at this point. Loosely overlapping characteristics connect certain aspects of the Mystery Schools with those of the mythic Hero/ine's Journey (the seeker and the quest, the arduous journey throughout which much is concealed, and the discipline and wisdom which emerge out of the challenges), as I will discuss in Chapter Twelve.

Themes at the Thresholds of the Mysteries

However the ancient schools were structured, and whatever the number of Gates to traverse or thresholds to cross, there appear to be common themes from past to present. (These same themes also appear, as I describe later, in my year of Sacred Dreaming.) Scholar-students in the Mystery Schools learned:

- To comprehend the art and science of Magic as an undefinable force that undergirds all reality; George G. M. James, in *Stolen Legacy,* calls the Egyptian priests, for example, "masters of magic" who "exercised control over the laws of nature";
- To become learned in mathematical systems, especially as these related to planetary spheres and other natural organizations;
- To awaken the receptive heart (without which the practices of love, compassion and forgiveness are not possible);
- To find purposeful existence for human betterment;
- To understand how Microcosm mirrors Macrocosm, and how the conscious and unconscious integrate visible and invisible worlds;
- To accept the power of thoughts to create realities (manifestation);
- To know that neither time nor space exist separate from cultural constructs;
- To experience at the Ninth Gate, or final threshold, a transcendent capstone event that replicated death and resurrection (involving a trance state, induced by meditation and fasting), during which the initiate encounters and learns—in a dreamlike or visionary state—from Cosmic Masters. Often this event lasted three days in earthly time, with obvious parallels to other resurrection stories;
- Accepting that All is One.

Are not these the same matters which concern us now in the enlargement of our consciousness? Within our minds, and in this moment, we are each creating and pursuing the processes and knowledge of the Mystery Schools, whether we are aware of it or not. The ancient quest still calls to you and to me.

53

Let's dispel a prominent, contemporary misconception about this search. Perceptions and misconceptions surrounding New Age thinking and New Thought systems may suggest that these spiritual concepts, including mystical ideas, are flaky, lacking rigor and precision. Although frequently tarred with such judgments, Mysticism is not a form of intellectual ectoplasm, morphing into squiggly theories. On the contrary, mystical study for thousands of years has been regarded as a sacred endeavor, requiring discipline, extensive higher learning, synthesis of all knowledge, perseverance, mental and emotional precision, as well as courage. As the scholar W. T. Stace points out in *The Teachings of the Mystics,* Mysticism should not be associated with concepts that are "misty, foggy, vague, or sloppy."

The Egyptian priests and other learned ones understood, as a matter of *fact*, that gods and goddesses were visible in the world and could be communicated with: "As above, so below." Those mystic practitioners of the super-physical possessed a profound comprehension of natural law, "could levitate, handle fire, live under water, sustain great pressure, harmlessly suffer mutilation, read the past, foretell the future, make themselves invisible, and cure disease," the Greek historian Proclus wrote. Even if we do not take Proclus's words at face value, the possibility that there are no boundaries between dimensions or between the visible and invisible worlds places us on a psychic and esoteric plane where the human mind can travel without barriers, and the great Mysteries are accessible to each of us.

Such concepts also illuminate the role of the Hierophant, that individual "who interprets sacred mysteries or esoteric principles," and who has successfully transited all levels of the Mysteries. He (since usually only men participated in these Schools) then becomes, in turn, the wise "explainer of the Mysteries." (Only the initiates in progress through the levels of learning were privy to those teachings.) It is interesting that the Hierophant is also usually one of the astral cards of the tarot deck; although the origin of tarot is obscure, many symbols of the Mystery Schools were incorporated into the mythology of the cards. The suits of the cards, as an illustration, are hierarchical in value, perhaps representing ascending levels of prophetic power (similar to the Mystery Schools). Like certain other esoteric practices ("Calling Down the Moon," visioning, skrying, as illustrations), tarot practice has been reduced to the derogatory term "fortunetelling," a current designation not indicative of sacred knowledge, but of sham and fraud. In like manner, the veneration of Magic as a worthy Art of the Supernatural or occult, and Magicians as holy practitioners of this art, has been diminished to children's entertainment at birthday parties. It is to be expected in our culture, then, that spiritual mysteries and paranormal realities are often not taken seriously.

Yet Mysticism and the Mystery Schools are significant concepts for the modern spiritual seeker, and for this narrative. By limiting possibilities, dismissing mysterious events or dreams as meaningless, and misjudging experiences we do not understand, we cage the psychospiritual capacities of our minds.

Reflections: Chapter Five

The reflective comments for this chapter are shaped by referring to Neale Walsch's book, *Conversations with God: An Uncommon Dialogue*, first published in 1995. Although many critics and readers were/are skeptical, that single book turned into a series of more than nine sequential publications. If you are having difficulty working with the concepts of Mysticism, let's try to reframe it within whatever faith, atheistic, or agnostic context works best for you.

1. Using the perspective of having an "uncommon dialogue" with an infinite Force, entity, or imaginative figure, start by writing down five descriptive words or phrases which apply to that Being (e.g., "all powerful"). After defining characteristics of the Force, describe your discomfort or comfort level with these concepts. Or write whatever you want to express about this hypothetical dialogue.
2. If you could talk to this Divine Entity, what three important questions would you want to ask? You may wish to reread your

questions two or three times to fix them in your mind, in order to think about them as you go about the tasks of daily life, prior to doing this exercise. Treat this as a serious inquiry, not a trifling activity. Remember, you are creating the curriculum of your own sacred Mystery School as you respond to each chapter's Reflections.

3. Go into a space of calm breathing for about two minutes, eyes closed, and then imagine you are actually having that "conversation with God," or whatever Divine Energy you are drawn to. Participate in that conversation (eyes remaining closed) for ten minutes. After the awkward sense of doing something artificial passes, how does it feel to be conversing with a Cosmic Intelligence?

4. Has this exercise widened your perspectives about mystical realities? Journal specifically about how or whether your perceptions have shifted.

CHAPTER SIX

What Is True?

A year after the events at Karnak, when I finally met with the scholar-teacher Robert Masters at his home in Pomona, New York, I shared my passionate story about Karnak and Sekhmet with him. Bob gazed probingly at me, and then nodded. He understood. That first day began his mentoring and teaching of me. He initiated a cumulative and increasingly difficult psycho-spiritual curriculum of research, journaling, and actions, most of which will be shared with you throughout this narrative.

Bob assured me these experiences with Beloved Sekhmet (She *had* become my Beloved) were not uncommon. In his communication with individuals across the globe who shared their Sekhmet stories with him, similar experiences were related—especially the power of her awe-full energy. Because Bob was a leading Sekhmet scholar, as well as a practitioner of Her devotion, he was at that time a major source of knowledge about this Goddess. From around the world, people who had encountered Her mysterious Being reached out to him for keys to understanding their experiences.

"Sekhmet seizes and claims you," he explained to me, his tone respectful of this miracle; he was reverent, but also matter-of-fact. "Those are the words all of us use to describe our experience—*seized* and *claimed*."

Indeed, I had not imagined Her!

What Is True?

To return to the basic question that opens this chapter: What is true? There is no provable answer in this physical sphere; Truth is all about perception. To a degree, it is about our belief systems and how we expect things to feel or to be. If I anticipate witnessing a ghost in a legendary haunted house, I probably will see one. If only my rational mind is in gear, I most likely won't see the ghost. Let me demonstrate with another anecdote.

Following an invitational spiritual conference I hosted in my Ohio home, the attendees asked to visit the Sekhmet Room, a sacred area that—no matter where I have lived—is always set aside in my home for meditation and devotion. One of the guests told me after leaving the space, "I hate to tell you this, but I didn't feel anything." That was her reaction.

On the other hand, another of my colleagues, who walked into the Sekhmet Room five minutes later, had a radically different reaction. He stopped dead still in the doorway before backing away.

"Yowee!" he exclaimed. "I've never felt anything like this before—waves of energy coming at me. Sekhmet's really there!"

This was a man not given to overreaction, who had studied with many spiritual leaders and had never before (he told me) felt such a strong spiritual Presence. Before leaving my home, he asked for additional time alone with Sekhmet.

"Go for it!" I told him.

Although he spent a solitary half-hour with Sekhmet, he said afterwards, with disappointment, "She told me She is not the One I'm seeking."

Same sacred room, same time frame, and two wildly different reactions. Each one believed in their comment. Was Sekhmet's energy there, or not? What is true? That ambiguity seems to be a pattern with a Sacred Being; each of us has to experience our own encounter, interpret the event, and name it true or not.

58

Musing about Truth, we can think about two different, yet similar, myths: the Voyages of Ulysses and the Earthly Journey of Christ. (Because speaking of the latter as a myth may be disturbing to some of you, I define *myth* in this context as a story that seeks to describe the nature of a particular Truth.)

Both external tales are epic adventures of heroic human figures whose exploits are at one and the same time mortal and immortal. Ulysses, although not immortal, possesses at times supernatural power and is aided by the Goddess Athena. The mortal story is what happened on the external quest (but is it true?), while the immortal (spiritual) narrative is what it means—or could mean (is it true in the metaphysical sense?). In each case, the tales can be broadly seen as the quest for our universal home. The hero of each story returns at last, after suffering and triumph, to an earthly (Ulysses) or a heavenly (Jesus) home. As seekers (not everyone chooses the quest), perhaps we each seek, at the end of our journeys, our place of psychic safety and rest, our universal home. What is true may be simply what each of us internally finds to be true, as we also find the Divine within ourselves. So Jesus may be the Savior of humankind, a prototype of a more evolved race to come, or simply a man of immense faith and compassion, who may or may not have been a God Incarnate, when he lived two millennia ago. Is Ulysses the great hero who overcame all obstacles to govern his people wisely, or is he the darker figure of *The Iliad* who kills his own son? If both aspects of his behavior existed, at least metaphorically: What is true?

A parable is told about the nineteenth-century writers Herman Melville and Ralph Waldo Emerson. Great companions, they frequently walked together in the woods around Concord, Massachusetts. It is said that during their walks Melville saw only the shadows of the forest, while Emerson saw only the light falling through the trees. Which perception is true? In each case, each author lived out and wrote about the thematic realities he observed.

More to the point: If spiritual Truth exists, may we understand it? Is Sacred Presence real? Within this narrative of a powerful God-Being, is Sekhmet true? Did She claim and seize me?

She did! The truth of Her Presence throughout these years is as real to me as my own breath. I have felt her, glimpsed the Goddess in Her many appearances, seen Her in visions, heard Her wisdom, lived through multiple synchronicities, and dreamed Her dreams. For me, there is no Truth more vibrant than this. The results of the Goddess's guidance in my life have led to a multitude of shifts in consciousness. A different person than I was, wiser and more aware of the gift of Sekhmet's presence, I can now define my own experiences of different realities. These definitions, however, may not match yours. Which definition is true?

In the beginning, I occasionally wondered if this connection with a Divine Energy was a bit of madness—perhaps even a great deal of madness. I did not know then what I now know well: many people walk with their God/dess Beings and have been in the Living Presence of the Divine, here and now—not just in the historical accounts of past mystics. Numbers of these individuals have also had moments of concern for their sanity. In her DVD on *Spiritual Madness*, Caroline Myss associates such deep questioning with the mystical dark night of the soul, an experience usually essential to spiritual transformation, as well as to coming to peace with enigmatic questions, such as: what is true?

Sekhmet's compelling presence in my life has taught me that rules other than reason apply to the esoteric dimensions of our lives. Given that perception, I will share another strange happening with you. This event is straightforward and yet uncanny. It illustrates the constant, immediate presence of great Spiritual Forces, and their split-second interventions in our lives. It also affirms that other norms and other realities most likely do exist and, more often than we recognize, affect our daily experiences.

One wintry night, seven months after Karnak and while I was still in Massachusetts, I was driving on ice, about to make a right turn at a busy intersection. Although I checked for traffic, I did not see the dark automobile racing down the road until we were about to crash. I only had time to think, "This is going to be *ba-a-d!*" when I felt my car literally lifted out of the way and placed back on the road after the speeding auto had passed. The experience happened so fast it seemed almost casual. Nevertheless, in that split second, I fleetingly saw four angels pick my vehicle up—and then the event was over.

Accepting the Esoteric

Like you, perhaps, I have sometimes tried to govern my decisions solely from my rational mind, as the trained teacher and scholar I am. Nevertheless, after Sekhmet appeared—and following the myriad of seemingly irrational experiences I encountered—I realized that an intellectual-emotional equilibrium is not always possible or desirable in decoding these Mysteries. Spiritual conviction is required to metaphorically let go of the trapeze bar of reason and fly through the air without a net to grab onto the bar of Mysticism coming toward me. But I did make that leap. How could I not?

Sekhmet continues Her presence in my life. My conviction about her guiding presence is reaffirmed by recent books by Eben Alexander, MD, and Roisin Fitzgerald (corporate executive turned artist and author), as well as others who have shared mystic experiences. (Both Alexander and Roisin had near-death experiences.) Each of them describes similar mystical happenings, using the same descriptive language as I do. True or not in worldly perceptions, we each lived through events that cannot adequately be named, or unanimously agreed to, by those who have not experienced such radical reality.

Yes, that event of angels lifting up my car was alive for me—and certainly my car was moved out of harm's way—but a larger perception was present. A psychic, supernormal portal swung open in my consciousness. My experience was from a reality beyond this physical world. It was simultaneous and synchronized by the merging of dimensions. I was granted an insight into awarenesses later affirmed by my connection with Sekhmet. The realms we see are a small slice of the Divine Energies and vast consciousness that are possible for each of us to experience. As we seek authenticity, identity and our Divinity within, as we expand our souls' knowledge (our reason for being born into the physical realm), we develop the capacity to perceive the blended realities of the invisible with the visible. Truly, All Is One.

Consider that the query posed in this chapter continues as a subtext to this entire narrative. It permeates every description and metaphysical theory presented. Perhaps, after all, possible answers to the question of "What is true?" are found in two other questions: "What is the mind of God?" and "What is the Divine within the mind of each of us?"

Reflections: Chapter Six

There is only one query for this Reflection:

1. In whatever context you wish, consider this: What is the Divine within your mind?

CHAPTER SEVEN

My Spiritual Neter

Bob Masters was my profound teacher. The experience of being seized and claimed by Sekhmet, as well as the extended scenarios of the Dreaming Time (described later in this narrative), would not have been intelligible without his guidance. Even with his reflective questions and observations, the meaning of the dreams remained elusive and puzzling at times. As we learn from the numerous dream accounts in the Bible, sequential dreams often present parables to be deciphered by the dreamer, as is the case in Joseph's story of Egypt's seven years of plenty, followed by seven years of drought.

How did I finally have the good fortune to share a personal conversation with the reclusive Robert Masters? Where had I finally found the boldness to connect with this reclusive scholar, and how had I attracted his interest? As is usually the case with Sekhmet, there is a story to tell. I had been reticent about contacting Bob, even after reading his landmark book, wary of his cautions about working with the Goddess, and uncertain that my experience at Karnak was worthy of his attention. Because of his reputation, I also thought it would be impossible to meet him. Little did I know what events lay ahead!

The synchronicities unfolded in this way. A year after Karnak, I was living in California while Dr. Masters, with his wife Dr. Jean Houston (also an iconic author and teacher), lived on the opposite coast. None of us had ever met, and the geographic distance was daunting; this was years before the Internet became so dominant in all our lives. At the same time, I was still tentatively finding my way with this Goddess, unsure of the outcome if I opened a connection with

Bob. In my naiveté, I did not yet comprehend the power of Sekhmet to arrange all things for Her spiritual purposes, a power She continues to demonstrate in my life.

Readers may wonder why I was slow to grasp the profound grace of Sekhmet's appearances. Although the astonishing gift had continued, I was still hesitant about its meaning. Let me tell you that the presence of the Living God/dess, whatever that Divine Being may be named, is incandescent, electric with awe. Remember Biblical descriptions of the angel's appearance to Ann, the mother of Mary, and later the Annunciation to Mary of her destiny? The women reacted with terror, angelic or Divine power being almost too much for humans to endure.

"Oh, just get on with it!" you may be thinking. Let me explain. Translate the appearance of angels to Sekhmet, an ancient Being roaming the desert before Jehovah existed in human thought. Understand that these sacred forms *are* unfathomable *energy*, nonphysical energy, outside of anything we understand. Perhaps, in that context, my ambivalence makes more sense.

A Timeline of Connections

At this stage in the narration, outlining a brief chronology of events would be helpful for the reader. Sekhmet revealed Herself to me at Karnak in March 1995. I moved to California in February 1996, the extended Dreaming Time started in late March of that year, and I first met Dr. Masters that June. I started working closely with him and with Dr. Houston during the late summer and winter of 1996–97, travelling often on weekends to stay at their home in Pomona, New York.

Access to these two great minds occurred because Sekhmet implemented another of Her intricate cycles of synchronicity. One sunny afternoon, as I was driving in downtown San Francisco on my way to an appointment, I realized too late that a speeding car had gone through the red light at a four-way intersection. Just before the collision, I heard Sekhmet saying in my head, "Don't be afraid. You will not be harmed." With those words, I relaxed as my SUV was struck and rolled over one and one-half times, sparks cascading from metal grinding across pavement.

When the automobile came to rest on its roof, I heard voices saying, "Is she still alive? Call 911!"

Although the car was totaled, I walked away without the proverbial scratch. As Sekhmet had assured me, I had not been harmed.

That jarring experience, however, got my attention as I anticipated the inevitable next steps to be revealed. By now I knew when Sekhmet was at work in my life. The following morning, I had a networking appointment with a woman whom I had never met, but whose coaching work was similar to mine. Mutual friends had connected us. Because my soon-to-be-acquaintance, Judith, had taken several seminars with Jean Houston and knew Bob as well, I looked forward to our meeting,

When I opened the door to Judith, she looked at me, paused for a beat, and then said, "I had the weirdest experience meditating this morning; the thought just came into my head that I was supposed to give you this." She knew nothing about my experiences with Sekhmet or my metaphysical interest in Bob. "Here," she said, handing me Bob Masters's card with his home phone number.

Astonished, I took the card. By now, however, the previous day's accident and all the other amazing events evolving in my life had prepared me simply to roll with whatever coincidence occurred.

"I think this is a sign that I can talk honestly with you," I told her. "What a crazy story I have to tell you about Egypt!"

Judith put an arm around my shoulder. "Nothing is crazy when you deal with the metaphysical. That's why I always follow my intuition; otherwise, I would never have brought Bob's card with me today."

Thus, Sekhmet (with Judith's assistance) led me to Robert Masters.

After Judith left that afternoon, I took Bob's card off the mantel and held it, as elation bubbled up inside of me. I had been asking Sekhmet to bring me to Bob, and now I requested that She guide my words and actions. After rehearsing what I would say to introduce myself, I called Dr. Masters (it took me months to ease into calling him the more familiar "Bob").

Of course, he did not answer the call himself. His assistant talked with me first, asked me questions about my purpose in speaking with him, and promised that she would call me back within the next day or two. When the return call came, it was Bob's voice I heard on the line. This was the revered man himself, the scholar who had spent his life studying about and encountering the powerful Sekhmet! His deep, resonant voice was just what I had expected from a man who walked with this Goddess.

Although the phone conversation was easy, his requirements before meeting me were not. He requested a complete description of every Sekhmet contact, the specific event precipitating my call, and the reasons why I thought these would be of interest to him. He was interested only in those individuals, he told me, whose experiences with Her were unique. I hoped that I would soon be numbered in that select group. Two weeks later, after reading my descriptions, he asked for a photograph, just a head shot, to meditate on. Only when he was satisfied of my bona fides with the Goddess did he invite me to meet him.

Mystagogue as Mentor-Teacher

I flew out to visit Bob at his and Jean's museum of a home in Pomona. As the main door opened, I was greeted by Bob and two life-sized wooden carvings of Sekhmet and Athena (Jean's archetype), who welcomed visitors into a long room filled with antiquities, inviting seating arrangements for conversations, and a massive fireplace at the far end. Imagine my curiosity! The house was everywhere crowded with surprises: a suit of armor, broken pieces of ancient statues, innumerable books, antique Persian rugs, a spiral staircase, and a great tower room holding additional antiquities, where Jean wrote, meditated, and worked. Bob's private chamber for Sekhmet was on the second floor, a space opened only to his most trusted colleagues and mentees.

The pièce de résistance, in the place of honor in Bob's work area, was a medium-sized bronze statue, thousands of years old, of Sekhmet.

Seated with staff and ankh, the statue was an inspirited figure (that is, Her sacred spirit had been ritually invoked in the statue by Egyptian priests eons ago, and by Bob more recently), gleaming with a bronze patina. According to its provenance, the statue had been used by priests of Ancient Egypt in their temple work: Sekhmet, among Her many attributes, is the Goddess of healing and magic. Many times over the years to come, in Pomona and later in Oregon, I had the privilege of long, private meditations in front of this sacred figure.

Sekhmet has transfixed many a human being over the centuries; I was not the first nor the last to be enthralled. When the well-known anthropologist, Margaret Mead, saw the figure for the first time, she, too, was struck by its commanding presence. As Robert Masters tells it, Mead spoke often of the statue's embedded power, and later "developed her own strong affinity for Sekhmet."

There is a mysterious coda to the tale of this statue, the kind of final event out of which myths are spun. At Bob's memorial service, this sacred statue—in perfect condition—was brought to the gathering as part of the remembrance ceremony. There, it suddenly broke into thirty pieces.

In the atmospheric setting of the Pomona house, during visits that went on intermittently across a number of years, I worked with Robert Masters as my Neter (an ancient term for Divine mentor-teacher), and also grew to know Jean Houston. My experience with each of them was markedly different. Although they had been co-researchers and writers earlier in their careers, they had different academic training and scholarly interests. Bob's focus was on Sekhmet's powers, what lost knowledge we could glean from the history and myths of this Goddess, and Her relevance to the modern world. Jean's expertise, on the other hand, was the study of human development, myths, and archetypes, as well as transformational action in the world. She had worked closely with Joseph Campbell and Margaret Mead (who "adopted" Jean as her other daughter), among other admired figures. In particular, Jean helped me find comfort in the many challenges of working with Sekhmet and in placing Her powerful presence within larger archetypal patterns.

In these ways, Bob's and Jean's generous mentoring provided a context for illuminating the meaning of Sekhmet's presence and my journey with Her, as well as for my growing spiritual awareness. Each of them was instrumental in understanding my extended experiences with Sacred Dreams, along with the realization of the dreams' significance. Of course, I grew to love them both dearly.

When I reread in my journals the descriptions of my dreams, conversations with Bob and Jean, and other esoteric events, the meanings sometimes shimmer away, will-o'-the-wisps. Truth is embedded, but it remains partially hidden; fragmentary understanding, not full disclosure, may be all that is granted. Often in mythic tales, dreams are riddles to which the seeker must find answers.

As a reader, you are experiencing this narrative on the page from outside in, whereas I am telling it from inside out. I am the dreamer explaining events both personal and supernatural, whereas you are the spectator-reader who seeks the meanings of these happenings in order to apply those meanings to your own life. My challenge is to bring you into this reality, inviting your engagement, too, with other dimensions. You and I are both on the frontier of an unmapped country as we encounter the Mysteries of Sekhmet—or any other supernatural Presence. This is a moment for "a willing suspension of disbelief." Although I can offer you my answers to these riddles, impenetrable Mysteries. *Tell all the Truth but tell it slant,* as the poet Emily Dickinson tells us. The Truth is not just slant; it is often impermeable.

To convey the full range of strange events—as Bob Masters recommended—I followed a disciplined routine of recording both substantive and subjective details from my recollection of these experiences. The practice of immediate journaling—before ideas, details, settings, emotions can be lost—reminds us that contact with Divine Beings is never to be taken lightly. The discipline of journaling trains our memory for astute observation and sharp recall; in time, it becomes a sacred practice. By writing down our experiences, we involve sensory recall (sight, feeling, hearing, and so on) that intensifies the processes of comprehension and transformation. The mystical is, then, informed by practice.

Bob Masters described his book on Sekhmet "as a scriptural work" in which he calls for "the need to Multiply the Images of Sekhmet." Devoted to the Goddess throughout his life, his vision encompassed a cosmology within which each of us is embedded with an internal authority to interpret all aspects of spiritual and esoteric knowledge. Dr. Masters' Sekhmet book, reintroducing this Goddess to the world, is intended to be, in his words:

> . . . a means by which a Nonhuman Being of the Order of Beings known as Gods and Goddesses manifests to humans in a way suited to the present consciousness of humans. Understand that such works penetrate into the whole Being—body and mind and spirit, conscious and unconscious, cells and souls.

Such eloquent language can only come from the heart and mind of a visionary who has witnessed elements of the Mysteries while still dwelling in his *humanness*. To paraphrase his perceptions: to know Sekhmet (or the Divine Beloved) is to know the nature of All That Is. She *is* the Mystery, as I repeat several times in this narrative. "At the end, I am That Which you seek," proclaims an ancient invocation to the Goddess.

Reverently Seeking the Divine

As William James explains, a mystical experience is transitory; our human challenge is to capture its wonder on the page before it completely dissipates. How frustrating it is not to possess language apt enough, or powerful enough, to recreate mystical meaning from the event. Sometimes, spiritual insight arises out of a mental recall process that strums the strings of sympathetic vibrations between the remembered events and our capacity to understand them. This resonance also takes the form of that prime intuition that is beyond reason. At a visceral level, we can then *feel* and *know* the existence of sacred realities and dimensions.

One of Bob's most important teachings was his caution to be scrupulous about discerning the difference between Dream Truth and my own desires and psychological "stuff." Not only did he mentor me through spiritual exercises to develop intuition, psychic awareness, and explore my *chai*, but we worked with past life regressions, meditation, and memory recall.

"Take in as much of each experience as you can safely handle, since you have merely begun the esoteric initiation," he said. "Remember: the Power of Divine Beings is unimaginable; understand that you can be burned to a crisp by that energy. You may think that's an exaggeration, but it is not. Don't misuse this Force or get ahead of yourself."

He made a gesture of pressing his fingers against his Third Eye as he swiveled his chair to look out the window of his office.

"In other words, don't attempt a ritual beyond your knowledge. Treat all things Spiritual with supreme reverence, and respect the risk you may be taking. Reality is tricky, with many aspects. The human race exists in a never-ending conflict between the Forces of Light and the Forces of Darkness, as it ever has been."

After a pause he added, "There is so much we don't know, don't comprehend."

In making those comments, Bob was musing upon his own experience. When he was an early practitioner of his Spiritual Craft, Bob told me, he attempted a metaphysical ritual that shredded the veil between this dimensional reality and unknowable realms. What he saw and experienced was a paranormal event so terrifying that his mental stability was at risk for weeks. Without the pan-dimensional wisdom of his wife, Jean Houston, he told me, he would have lost his sanity.

"Prepare yourself mentally and emotionally for every ritual and reflection you do; never venture into worlds you aren't ready for," he repeated.

"Tell me more," I said.

"Bizarre encounters have happened to many Seekers, Mystics, sacred Magicians," he cautioned. "They do not always return to sanity. We cannot imagine what is behind the veil, and a glimpse of it can be transcendent, or it can horrify beyond our understanding, depending on circumstances. None of us really knows how to control those circumstances."

Giving me time to absorb these comments, Bob continued, "Treat Her power with absolute respect. She wouldn't willingly destroy you, but God-Beings don't always comprehend their power or the constraints of what we humans can and cannot handle—especially when we have been seized."

As I recalled how terrifying—and yet how luminous—was Sekhmet's appearance at Karnak, I understood his words. For those readers who desire to invite mystical experiences into their lives, I ask you, too, to be aware of the unlimited power of Divine Presence. Although unconditional love surrounds us, so do the darker dimensions of our own spiritual ignorance, as well as metaphysical realms and energies we cannot comprehend. Divine illumination, splendid and enthralling, also possesses scorching intensity.

Bob's wise words were not an exaggeration. As I participated later in Jean's seminars and workshops, I heard similar stories from other seekers. I will relate one of those, the aftermath of which I had firsthand knowledge. A physics faculty member at a Midwestern university where I was provost a number of years ago had experimented with esoteric rituals over the years. A proclaimed atheist, he invited his students to participate outside of class in metaphysical experiments exploring other dimensions. Given today's scientific advancements, we might categorize the experiments as aspects of quantum physics.

One night, he and a small group of students, outside the classroom, performed an edgy physics experiment. An event so grotesque occurred that he and his students were horrified. As a result of that incident, he abandoned his study of other dimensions and converted to Christian fundamentalism. When he and I discussed this event a year later, he told me he was still unable to describe the experience without apprehension. As he grimaced, the look on his face was convincing enough.

Energy of Soul

As discussed in Chapter One, the New Science is blurring boundaries that for thousands of years have separated dimensions and realities, as well as dividing human beings from the power of their own conscious-ness. If everything is energy at the quantum level, then the Unified Field is indeed the Field of All Possibilities. On the border of the shrink-ing divide between infinite and human realms, Sekhmet had claimed me with compelling power. Some of us who have been seized by this Goddess refer to the event as being "Sekhmeted."

The dynamism of universal energy also draws all living creatures and objects into fields of similar energy vibrations. Within the context of Sekhmet's Divine Design, Bob Masters and I had to meet so that he could take on the role of Neter to my neophyte translation of esoteric occurrences. We were linked through our energetic connection with Sekhmet.

By the time the Venerable Bob, as I called him, became my Neter, I was eager for a wider understanding of the dreams and all the Sekhmet scenarios, as well as to comprehend the Neter's role in my experiences. In his book *The Goddess Sekhmet,* Bob defines Neter in this way:

> *This term is most often reserved for God and Goddesses but can also be properly applied to some other higher and more subtle beings. As the pupil progresses along a spiritual Path, he/she eventually reaches a point beyond which no further progress is possible unless the teacher is a* Neter. *The* Neter *teaches and demonstrates in ways that no human teacher is able to do. Magical and spiritual disciplines done—or attempted to be done—without the guidance of the* Neters *were labeled "Paths of Fools" in most ancient traditions.*

Such words are a reminder of the tale already shared with you about the esoterically untutored, risk-taking faculty member who unexpect-edly confronted the terrible Unknown. Such warning stories exist for a reason.

When Sekhmet first brought me to Dr. Robert Masters in June of 1996, I intuitively trusted his wisdom. He was an Old Soul to whom She had given the task of tutoring me, reassuring me about the eso-teric experiences I was encountering, and introducing me to sources of knowledge about Her. Revisiting my Dream Journals before writing these chapters, I am again grateful for that guidance. The journals are fascinating as they reveal a great Goddess in action, and they are also daunting. Without a Neter, my passage into a different consciousness would have been far more difficult—perhaps even more dangerous. Being claimed by this powerful and paradoxical Goddess shocked my psyche. I was a sophisticated woman, but I was such a neophyte in the realms of the supernatural. Although I had received paranormal experiences before, nothing had reached this pitch of intensity. I was being swept up in a miracle.

The Sacred Dreams were part of that miracle. Initiating my active spiritual journey into a strange land, they also defined possibilities for action within that new geography. Sekhmet is not a passive Goddess, and those of us called to Her are not allowed to glide through our choices. We have "purposes supreme" (as one of my minister friends terms it) that we must fulfill. This passionate Goddess seizes and calls us to the work of transformation, to name and to act upon the "Possible Impossible." The Wizard (teacher, shaman, artist) within us is ignited by that call, and the Fire in the Soul must be answered with corresponding passion.

One of the initial questions Bob asked me was whether other Great Beings had appeared to me. Sekhmet, as already mentioned, was not the first Divine Being to visit me over the years before Karnak, although She was certainly the most compelling! Her declaration, "I claim you!" was decisive. However, dream appearances by Isis and Hecate the year before my trip to Egypt presaged—like previews of coming attractions—the appearance of Sekhmet, as well as my awakened consciousness. When I shared these past events with Bob, he explained that Hecate and Sekhmet share the same energy and are sometimes equated; this was new information for me. The Hecate dreams, he suggested, were intended to prepare my unconscious mind for Sekhmet's later dream extravaganza.

"Hecate may have been opening the portal for Sekhmet—not that She needs help!" he laughed. Then he added, "Both Isis and Hecate are related to myths of transformation, death, and resurrection, fitting connections with Sekhmet."

It made sense, then, that these mystical appearances were linked. No spiritual action is ever wasted, and no spiritual event takes place in a vacuum. The transformations that accompany appearances of Sekhmet—or any other Divine Presences—are wild and dramatic: a corporate executive who leaves her position to devote her life to art, founding a studio and gallery in the process; a neurosurgeon who gives up medicine to become a teacher and speaker; a teacher who becomes an inspiring self-help guru, and so on. That which we have been in our lives, we cannot continue to be. We are directed by new imperatives. Although such imperatives are usually sweeping in scope, lesser imperatives are also contained within the whirlwind of life changes.

Since energy is the driving force of all things, we humans are mutually and magnetically attracted to the energy of other beings, our four-footed companions among them. Human curiosity about our interaction with mammalian intelligence and energy is as ancient as cave drawings, many of which suggest that animals—hunted by necessity—were also revered for their spiritual aura by early humans. Accepting that elephants, chimpanzees, dolphins, and whales, for instance, possess large brains capable of intelligent reasoning and loving emotions, creates another paradigm shift in the nature of consciousness, a shift suggesting that there is no hierarchy of creation granting us superiority over other creatures.

Many of us, whatever descriptive language we may use, have encountered animal teachers, "friends of my soul" (as Jean Houston calls them), who have demonstrated immense powers of presence. One of these mystic animals was my wise canine companion, Bear.

Just as Sekhmet had brought Bob, Jean, and me into the same vibrational circle, She brought Bear into my life as my most important animal guide. (I can't resist this aside: Bear looked just like a wolf, my wolf totem animal reappearing, perhaps.) Bear and Bob mysteriously fit a similar energetic template: a bit rough around the edges, large and rugged, intelligent, fierce, and headstrong—qualities vibrantly Sekhmetian as well.

A rescue dog, he arrived in my life when he was five years old, already named "Bear." Because several home placements had ended in his return to the no-kill shelter, prospective adopters claiming he was too stubborn to be trained, he was skittish and defensive. Without question, however, I knew Bear was a soul gift from the Goddess when I found him at the shelter. As was true of many of Her gifts, Bear arrived with challenges. In order to remain together, my canine friend and I had to establish an equilibrium which would accommodate the psychic connection between us—this wild dog and this human who was still reeling from the mystical events that had begun at Karnak.

Working with a difficult-dog trainer, Bear and I tried to figure each other out. The Native American trainer, a gentle man in his eighties, told me repeatedly, "Tell Bear what you want from him. Say it over and over until he hears you. It's not the words, but your reassuring tone that he will understand."

Thus, I created a mantra that I repeated every day of his life for the next ten years: "Bear, I love you. Bear, I will never leave you. Bear, I am your home."

A magical transformation occurred during our fourth training session. Walking beside Bear on the deck of the trainer's house, I kept repeating those words aloud. Suddenly, Bear sat down on the wooden planks, staring at me with full attention, his dark eyes a well of intelligence. I concentrated on sending him the energy of my heart's intent until somehow our understandings merged. From that moment on, he and I had embarked on our long journey together. His stalwart companionship taught me trust and devotion, and I never doubted our psychic alignment. Respecting his animal wisdom was as essential to my spiritual growth as were my other insights. Instances of deep human-animal bonds are neither strange nor weird, and are part of the wide range of mystic phenomenon. Most of us have heard or read many such tales. I recall that Matthew Fox, the Episcopal priest who writes and teaches extensively about spiritual consciousness, sometimes referred to his dog as his spiritual advisor. Although the comment is tongue-in-cheek, it also makes a point about animal souls.

As I have already emphasized in this narrative, we need the comfort of a variety of communities as we travel our challenging spiritual paths. One of the laws of metaphysics, as we know, is that energetic vibrations attract similar vibrations, drawing other humans, Divine entities, and animal beings to our support—and drawing our support to them. We all need one another.

The night after Bear died, when my grief was still porous, he appeared in a dream, jumping ecstatically onto my bed, his arthritic body now lithe again, laughing with his tongue out (as he had laughed in life). Then he leaped over the headboard and through the wall into infinity. True to the end, he comforted my heart with one last message:

"I am happy. I am free. All is well."

Bear, too, was one of the Mysteries.

Reflections: Chapter Seven

Many of us have had a great teacher and/or a special animal in our lives. If we have been especially blessed, we have had both. The Reflection questions for this chapter focus on both.

1. If you had a Neter (or more than one) in your life, describe the individual(s). What characteristics set them apart for you?
2. What unforgettable impacts did they have on your life? Especially, how did they guide you in transforming your life?
3. Have you had a mystic dog or other animal in your life? Describe the animal's soul characteristics.
4. How did this mystic animal change your life?
5. What new understandings of reality, life, Spirit, and yourself occurred because of your Neter? Because of your special animal?

CHAPTER EIGHT

How Sekhmet Rolls

As I continued to learn from Bob Masters and Jean Houston, I flew once a month to New York to spend weekends with them. These times were my metaphysical tutorials. From mid-morning until early afternoon, I worked with Bob, including our informal lunches at the kitchen table, usually joined by Jean. Listening to their intelligent dialogues, which sometimes turned into quick-minded debates, I was invited to join in on topics ranging from DC politics (I was then directing an office in Washington during President Clinton's impeachment proceedings), to Joseph Campbell's theories, to pop music ("Walk Like an Egyptian"), to Egyptian history.

After lunch, Bob would retire for two or three hours, and I often spent that time alone with Jean, who—imparting her vast knowledge of nearly everything—opened to me perspectives of history, culture, and myth beyond my academic training. She was a mind-stretcher, as are all great teachers. She also had many questions for me about the Sekhmet events, and she shared some of her own experiences with this Goddess, as well as with her own archetype, Athena. In part, as a scholar of human development, she was intrigued by the stages and processes through which we mentally arrive at deep spiritual consciousness. Our human journey to such consciousness, a key theme in this narrative, is essential to Divine Being's connections with us. This is the reverberating meaning of my Sacred Dreams, as well as the continuing link between Sekhmet and my soul, as well your contact with the Divinity within you.

Throughout this narrative, I have portrayed Dr. Robert Masters as an iconic figure—and, on an archetypal level, he was that. There is an appropriate place for iconography in philosophy, literature, history, and other narratives. The energy of these larger-than-life figures is a high-voltage magnetism that draws us toward them. It's a common experience we have with master teachers. Since such figures teach and validate us, we trust their role in catalyzing our transformations. As my Neter, Bob affirmed my mystical experiences when I needed affirmation. In time, however, I needed to discover my own internal authority for Sekhmet's appearance in my life. As is true for each of us, standing in our own truth is a signifier of expanding consciousness.

Despite the breadth of his magnificent mind, however, Bob was as flawed as the rest of us. Perhaps, indeed, the magnitude of his imperfections may have been the flip side of his gifts. He could be angry, sarcastic, critical, dismissive, and indulgent in drink. He made missteps in his life, and he paid a price for those lapses. As he says in *The Goddess Sekhmet*, he was "chastened by Her," acknowledging that Sekhmet holds Her followers to demanding requirements of behavior and ethics.

Contemporary and historical examples abound of flawed leaders, women and men with their imperfections balanced by their accomplishments. Former President Bill Clinton, impeached for inappropriate sexual behavior, was nevertheless—as he has demonstrated during these past few years—a man of humanitarian conscience. Mother Teresa, a global spiritual teacher and minister to the poor, could also be manipulative and cunning when it served her causes. Winston Churchill was an alcoholic. Catherine the Great of Russia, involved in numerous shady political deeds, nevertheless strategically led Russia into the modern world.

I am making a spiritual point about imperfect human beings—like you and me—who nevertheless encounter Divine experiences with Sacred Beings. Whatever the condition of our individual spiritual evolution, a veil is sometimes lifted, and luminous Mysteries appear. It is to be hoped that exposure to sacred events leads us to greater consciousness, as well as to wiser hearts. Bob's shortcomings do not detract from his life purpose or the importance of his teaching. In like manner, our human imperfections do not barricade us from the

Source; rather, it is possible that our flawed, seeking selves may be the very human aspect that draws Spirit to us.

Although Bob Masters had a formative impact on my developing metaphysical awareness, Jean Houston also left an indelible imprint on my mind and heart. She, too, became my Great Teacher, as she is to this day. As the years have passed and I am truly coming home to myself, I still hear her wise, resonant voice delivering profound insights and asking unsettling questions, which even now impact my mind and heart, as is true for generations of her students and colleagues. She breathed life into our understanding that what the mind can visualize, it can also create. Thinking is an energetic action which dares us to manifest the "Possible Impossible." Dwelling in revelational times, as we do now, we are resonant to new discoveries about the capacity of our brains to change radically in the birth of new consciousness. As more information about quantum physics is available and as we experience our own esoteric events, we can understand how *The Art of Possibility* (the title of Rosamund Stone Zander's brilliant book) is emerging. Zander defines the path to Possibility as "restructuring meanings, creating visions, and establishing environments where possibility is spoken—where the buoyant force of possibility overcomes the pull of the *downward spiral*." If ever the world needed assistance to overcome the challenges of chaos and devolution ("the downward spiral"), it is now.

This is not beyond our imagination. The human mind has redesigned worlds of possibility in the past: the Golden Age of Greece and the Renaissance are examples that come immediately to mind. As reality is perceived in different ways, the boundaries between normal and paranormal shift to allow space for "restructuring meanings" and envisioning new paradigms. Consciously or not, this is the work each of us is now engaged in: the growing of consciousness to encompass shifting realities.

Power of Myth

While Bob, Jean, and I were working together, Bill Moyers was concluding his PBS series of interviews with Joseph Campbell about our human longing for myths and for templates, such as the Hero/ine's Journey, to interpret our experiences in the world. Listeners were enticed by Campbell's gift for storytelling as he reminded us that myths retold call out to our consciousness—as we know from the recurrence of themes, stories, and archetypal hero/ines since history began: the Savior, the Warrior King, the Amazon or Great Queen, the Scapegoat, the stories of resurrection, conversion (Saul on the Road to Damascus), the Great Flood, outcasts wandering on the desert or in the forests.

Myths are our cultural glue—the common language and narratives that bind our universal understanding. Through these stories, each of us can perceive ourselves in the mirror of all humankind. The stories also serve as a bridge to the mystical and supernatural: magic wands and swords, superpowered hero/ines, immortal beings, deities and demons, witches and ghosts. In our Western culture, who hasn't heard of Snow White, the Little Mermaid, Jack and the Beanstalk? Or Odin, Brunhilda, and the Valkyries of Scandinavian tales? Or more recently, Thor and the Avengers, as well as the many Super Heroes emerging to "save" a troubled world? Their miraculous stories pull us into imaginative dimensions, holding out the promise that magic may exist (the supernatural), lost treasures can be found, and we, too, can become hero/ines.

Mythic tales are also signifiers in comprehending Sekhmet, not only because She is a Divine Archetype who dares us to take Her journey, but because the stories surrounding this Goddess are universal. We can thrill to the image of the Divine Warrior who protects humankind from the Evil Ones; the Sacred Force who prevents destruction and war from overtaking us; the Great Lady whose fierce energy, even before acts of Divine Creation, stood between the human world and the realm of the Ur-Demons to preserve Order; the Luminous Healer who cures all pestilence; the Joyous Goddess who calls us to the Dance of Life; the Lady of Imagination, gifting us with the creative power of Her Fire, Passion, and Energy; the Magnificent One who nurtures us through all travails. To know the mythic, Divine Sekhmet is to know ourselves and the dream of ourselves.

Because spiritual processes are crucial to deeper understanding, we need soul companions with whom to converse. Dialogues with other scholars, teachers, and seekers unlock many Mysteries. Metaphysical isolation is quite different from individual journeying; it narrows the lens through which we see. In contrast, creating a network of trusted metaphysicians, shamans, mystics, and friends immeasurably enriches the conversations around, and contemplation of, the question that is recurrent in this narrative: What is True? (See Chapter 6.) Such companions serve, too, as metaphysical sounding boards for our burgeoning psyches. Time spent with key mentors, consequently, is precious—a safe zone where I can be open about my metaphysical life. Just as I talked with Bob as often as possible by phone, email, or in person, Jean Houston also visited me frequently in her travels. They were among the necessary companions of my soul. Yes, we are sometimes solitary travelers—as is required for reflection and self-discovery—but we go out from, and return to, communities.

The significance of questioning dialogue is illustrated by one of Jean's visits. I shared with her the latest news about my journey with Sekhmet. Several times a week for the past two months (this occurred almost a decade after the Dreaming Time), I told Jean that the Goddess had either made an appearance at my bedside and/or sent me new dreams. Obviously, She had a message for me—"I call you to a higher level," She beckoned—but I did not understand what "higher level" meant. Because you never ignore a Divine contact, I was troubled by my inability to figure it out. Even more troubling, I wondered whether I might be losing my open channel of communication with Her.

Jean listened intently before suggesting we meditate together in the Sekhmet Room. "When you need direction," Jean had taught me, "go into the silence and listen." When the meditation concluded, we both drew a releasing breath. Jean placed her hands on her knees and turned to me.

"She is asking you to be 'Sekhmet in the World,' " Jean said.

"I'm not sure I understand what that means."

"She wants you to be the physical body through which She can experience the sensations and earthly life that Her disembodied spirit cannot have without you," Jean explained.

I waited for the rest of it.

"And," Jean added, "She asks you to embody Her essence of love, compassion and resilience. *Be* Sekhmet."

Because this narrative is about diverse mystical and esoteric experiences, it's easy to forget that most of the ideas presented in this narrative are not really strange. They may appear so only because they are removed from a specifically Judeo-Christian context. Take the idea of Sekhmet in the World—or the indwelling Sekhmet, as an example. The concept is not as uncanny if we find common perceptual ground by comparing it to the many instances in the Bible where the believer is promised that God or Christ can be sought within. In the Book of Ezekiel, Jehovah promises, "I will put my Spirit within you and cause you to walk in my ways." In commenting about instances of such Divine action in the Bible, theologian R. A. Torrey speaks of how God "offers to form Christ in us by the power of His Holy Spirit . . . and to let this indwelling Christ live out His own life in us. . . ." Myths and dreams of many cultures have long established the concept of indwelling God/desses or Divine Beings. Indeed, ancient faith traditions—predating by centuries the rise of Christianity—permeate the emerging theologies that replaced the Old Religions. At certain of the famed, historic Temples, priestess-Goddesses (powerful women who held that designated position) presided over ceremonies; the indwelling spirits of Athena Polias at Athens, as well as Demeter and Kore at Eleusis, were integral to beliefs and rituals.

Within this frame, the idea of an indwelling Sekhmet slips easily into place. Moreover, the thought systems or paradigms of the normal and the paranormal are not so dissonant when their similarities are compared, rather than the contradictions magnified. If the miracles of the Bible—outside the boundaries of time/space/human and Divine—are believed to be supernaturally credible, then it stands to Possibility that other Mysteries are, too.

Reflections: Chapter Eight

For many readers, events such as I describe may appear foreign to your lives. But these mystical events are the sinew connecting esoteric possibilities, yours and mine.

1. This Reflection is intended to take you one step beyond the previous Reflections that asked you to hold a conversation with God. Since our journals grant us private space in which to be our authentic Selves (please protect the privacy of your writings by keeping them secure), dare to let go and think about how you would react to having a significant metaphysical experience today, in whatever form, with the Living Source. In a previous Reflection, you were asked to have a dialogue with Divinity. Now you are being asked to consider the emotional/psychic context of having such a living experience. Write down specific details of your reactions: trembling, ecstasy, fear, weeping, bodily shaking, a sense of being filled with light, and so on . If you have already encountered such a paranormal event, analyze its emotional impact more deeply.

2. How might this event or events change your perceptions of yourself and your own spiritual and life possibilities?

3. How might the previous questions assist your perceptions of "expanded consciousness"?

4. What is your reaction to "being (name the God-Being) in your life"? Do you feel responsible? Uneasy? Honored? Dismissive? Why?

5. Rosamund stone Zander, in her quote on p. 79 of this chapter, speaks of the "downward spiral." In the context of her comment, what does that phrase mean to you? And how does it affect your sense of possibilities within you?

A note to the reader about these questions: You may as well dive into the above Reflections, in addition to the previous ones. Now that you are validating your curiosity (or perhaps your own paranormal experiences) about the nature of mysterious spiritual experiences, you may even find that your own receptive curiosity flings you spontaneously into those esoteric realities. Stay open; allow the encounter(s) to happen. Then keep a record of them.

CHAPTER NINE

Leaping into the Deep

Every aspect of this book so far has prepared the reader for the core of this narrative: the Sacred Dreaming Time. Following the spiritual adventure at Karnak, a year of mystical dreams—sent and guided by Sekhmet—transformed every aspect of my life. Without warning, I was submerged nightly in paranormal experiences where the veil between daily existence and the arena of heightened supernaturalism was almost transparent. The spiritual energy surrounding and within the dreams was consuming.

I entitled this chapter "Leaping into the Deep" because the metaphorical image of jumping fearlessly into the Unknown captures the essence of the Mysteries, the Mythic Journey, and the wonder of Sekhmet's dreams. Since these concepts may not be common to your everyday knowledge (they certainly were not part of my ordinary thinking a few years ago), I have provided information elsewhere explaining Mysteries (Chapter 5) and Mythic Journeys (Chapter 13)— elements central, I believe, to defining the significance of my Sacred Dreaming Time.

More than simply providing information, however, it is important to compare the historical significance of these dreams to contemporary thinking about dream states. As is commonly known, ancient

---

Sekhmet at Karnak (**opposite**): Sandra Stanton, a Maine artist, painted this image. Sekhmet had visited her in a dream vision, inspiring her to create an earlier portrait of a dancing Sekhmet (a gift to Bob from the author and Merlinda Arnold, now owned by the estate of Dr. Robert Masters). I commissioned this second painting in Stanton's Sekhmet trilogy.

cultures—Egypt, Ancient Greece, Sumer, among many others—recognized the deeper meanings of dreams, rather than dismissing them as we frequently do in the modern world. Skeptical and cynical, we often make cocktail chatter out of dream interpretations and generally don't take dream realities seriously. But this attitude has not been true historically, since for thousands of years dreams were seen as messages of the gods. Ancient Egypt, as an illustration, produced the earliest known book containing dream messages, 1300 years before the birth of Christ. Many Bible passages pronounce the spiritual import of this activity (Numbers.12:6, e.g.): "Hear now my words. If there be a prophet among you, I the Lord will make myself known to him in a vision, and will speak to him in a dream." Along the same spectrum of sacred traditions, parts of the Qu'an were given to Mohammed in a dream. The bottom line of these examples is this credo: the Sacred speaks to us in dream time, and always has.

The cross-overs between dream and waking states of mind are phenomena known by all of us who dream (and we all do, whether we recall it or not), although modern thinking still questions the realities of dream worlds. One exception is Paracelsus, sixteenth century Swiss physician who, in his writings about philosophy and medicine, emphasized the value of dreams. One of his comments about external and internal realities could serve as a précis for this book:

> *That which the dream shows is the shadow of such wisdom as exists in man, even if during his waking state he may know nothing about it. . . .We do know it because we are fooling away our times with outward perishing things, and are asleep in regard to that which is real within ourself.*

This is certainly a description of *Finding the Divinity within Each of Us.* You may recall coming upon a similar statement by Chuang Tzu (China, fourth century, BC), one of the creators of Chinese Taoism, describing the conundrum of waking/dreaming realities: "I do not know whether I was then a man dreaming I was a butterfly, or whether I am now a butterfly dreaming I am a man." In more recent commentaries, the theories of Carl Jung and Freud throw us back again to a perception that dreams are essentially without value, psychological or otherwise. As Jung says, "the primitive" places a higher value on dreams than does "civilized man." He goes on to explain that the former:

> . . . *attributes an extraordinary importance to them, so that it often seems as though he were unable to distinguish between them and reality. To the civilized man dreams as a rule appear valueless, though there are some people who attach a great significance to certain dreams because of their weird and impressive character. This peculiarity lends plausibility to the view that dreams are inspirations.*

Jung's comments did serve the purpose of calling the public's attention back to the subject of dreaming, but his commentaries also added to the contemporary belief in dreams as nonsense. However, in the modern world, the difference between Eastern and Western cultures needs to be noted. Why dreams? If I had grown up in the East, the answer to "Why dreams?" would be self-evident. In many Eastern religions, dreams are windows to higher consciousness, a means of perceiving Invisible worlds, and insights into the Mysteries.

This brief discussion of dream interpretations, past to present, matters in the overarching paradigms of this narrative. The connection between dreams and Divine messages, the deeper truths of dream consciousness, and the esoteric validity of dreams are critical to your understanding of Sekhmet's presence and Sacred Wisdom.

My dream experiences began in earnest a year after my pilgrimage to Karnak. Perhaps catalyzed by my spiritual surrender to Her claiming me, Sekhmet visited me nightly, bringing vivid dreams filled with metaphors, narratives, vibrant images, serial narratives (as you will see in the Kwan Yin dreams, for example), and direct messages. My untutored reaction was simply to assume that these events were remarkable, but private, and to let them come and go. As I write this account now, I cannot believe I didn't comprehend at once this incredible window into mystical realities, as well as what a sacred gift She was offering me. Initially, my own sense of unworthiness got in the way. After you have received a revelatory occurrence, you, too, may be flooded with a similar sense. When a God-Being appears, it is shocking, and I could only wonder why these experiences were given to me. That reaction is a common response to a phenomenon about which we culturally also feel ambivalence.

Although the messages of dreams are significant in themselves, a larger meaning is usually at work. "The intensity of the experience seems to be measured by the way in which the individual's life is affected," observes mystic Alan G. Hefner. "No matter whether the experience is great or small, the life seems to be altered or reshaped in some way by it, and perhaps this itself is the mystical quality." The title of this chapter highlights that reality shift, from the surface to the depth of meaning, or—whatever the metaphor—to a transformation of life experience. "Leaping into the Deep," the Divine Voice calling within us as we jump, vivifies complete trust in Divine protection. Still, even as we trust, dreams still remain an enigma, as do the greater meanings of the Mysteries. Remember one definition of Mystery: "That which God alone knows and humans cannot know."

Dream Rituals

Rituals of lucid dreaming were not completely relevant to my experience, since Sekhmet's way was to catch me up immediately in a dream vortex in which I was powerless to do anything but experience and absorb the dreams. She had purpose and intent; I was her student/priestess/daughter. Because of that, She "directed" the scenarios like an orchestra conductor, demanding attention to the entire symphony and to every note. My dreams possessed shape like the complexities of a symphony: themes repeated, recurrent motifs, structure, directed creation.

Early in the process, the dreams also became interactive, rather than passive. Now Sekhmet had expectations of me to interpret the larger truth and prepare for bursts of new consciousness. My role was not simply to receive the nightly visions, but to understand and explicate the metaphysical content. I became the Hierophant myself for whom teaching and learning are evocative acts to be shared—as I am doing in this narrative. Normandi Ellis, whose book, *Imagining the World into Existence*, is relevant to our discussions throughout these chapters. Ellis makes this comment about Sekhmet, "She works with us in the dreamtime," and Her ancient dreams sometimes even contained spells to invoke Her presence. Without doubt, She used dreams, and continues to do so up to this very second, as a communication channel with Her human followers. Many of the mantras and exaltations to Her—from ancient fragments of temple rites and references in *The Book of the Dead* to contemporary invocations (such as those in *Heart of the Sun*)—acknowledge that She is the supreme granter of visions and sacred dreams. From the beginning of Her recognized existence (more than 5,000 years ago), She has sent her dreams to us, lightning bolts in the darkness.

Whatever the reader may believe about sacred dreams, if they appear in your life, they will possess authority and meaning different from ordinary dreams. Often, too, they will display a Divine imprint or signature (with Sekhmet, for instance, there is an abundance of red and gold colors, flashing light, and streams of energy). At times, you may hear internally, as I did, the God/dess's perpetual command, "Pay attention!"

Into the Deep of Teaching Dreams

As I began to record them in my journal, the dreams came thick and fast for nearly eleven months. They occurred every night, and often several times a day if I took short naps. Whenever I closed my eyes, the dreams would start. The experience was fabulous, in that sense of truly being fabled. Because I kept my journal notes after every dream, I *know* what happened. These experiences I share with you now are not reconstructed years after the fact; the journals are my source material, the still-fresh record written in the immediate aftermath of the experiences.

Bob told me once, "Very few people have spiritual encounters like this. Keep a written account of everything that appears in your dreams, no matter how insignificant you think the details are. Keep a pen and pad by the bed, as well as wherever you nap."

"What other things should I be aware of?" I asked him. The dreaming was a version of entering the Unknown; I had never realized such extended dreams were possible, just as I had never before realized that the mystical is so near to our consciousness.

"Put down the date, time, what She is wearing—the colors, jewelry, headdress, whether She holds a staff, who or what is around her, whether She is active or passive, and whatever else you notice. Write down details of the setting, every word, image, nuance, the tone of each dream. Do it immediately, before you get up to do anything else. Dreams are ephemeral and evaporate in the flick of an eye. While the dream is fresh, miss nothing."

"I don't always know what is important and what things don't matter," I said, "and some of the dreams are very long."

"Even if you don't understand it, write it down! What you don't know now may have meaning months or years from now. And always remember to thank Her for this great blessing."

Let's pause briefly on those last words. In dealing with spiritual entities, whatever knowledge or parts of the Mysteries they share with you, these insights are sacred gifts. Given freely to us, they are another signifier of Divine Presence in our lives. I urge that you always begin and end your meditations, prayers, dreaming times, with expressions of unreserved gratitude.

"There are a number of people who have had similar dreaming experiences with other God-Beings. But this is the first time I have ever heard of Sekhmet granting anyone this extended Dream Time," Bob continued. Then he reiterated, "Don't miss any detail—*write everything* down!"

As a reader, you must be curious about the dreams. What were they like—content, color, dialogue, geography, people in the scenarios? What did I understand at the time, and what do I better understand about them now, twenty years later? Since the dreams are a linked narrative (like scenes in a film or TV episode), and since Sekhmet used them as Teaching Dreams, these vivid mythic experiences deserve separate chapters (11 and 12).

The Dreaming Time lasted almost a year, a phenomenon in itself. The thematic message was often not shuttered, but direct. Sekhmet led me, as you will see, through a symbolic search for Enlightenment and Higher Consciousness (the Hero/ine's Journey). She also had another intention: to reveal Herself, Her living nature (including the paradoxes and contradictions inherent in our incomplete grasp of the Sacred). I witnessed Her love and compassion; fire, passion, and energy; healing power; magic used to restore and renew; radiance and splendor; all of the characteristics that have already been described in this narrative, and will be echoed again in different guises.

As the dreams went on, month after month, and as the Goddess was luminously *with* me, I was more tightly bound to Her than ever. On those rare occasions when neither Bob nor I could translate the meaning of a dream, he would say, "Read over your journals periodically so that you begin to see the entire pattern. Some meanings will emerge then that weren't apparent a few weeks ago, but are now evident. These are teaching dreams; she wants you to understand an accumulation of meaning over time."

Writing this book has been another numinous revelation. Two decades ago, these mystical events unfolded. As I examine now the typed transcriptions of my notes, some of the dreams come back to me with etched clarity, and many of them (such as the battlefield dreams described later) have accumulated new perspectives.

Multiple Divine Archetypes

It is important to mark the difference between the earlier appearance of Isis in my life and the event at Karnak four years later with Sekhmet. The nature of all Divine Light Beings is not the same. Although the core of unconditional love and compassion remains constant, each of the Sacred Ones manifests with unique energy and leaves a distinct impression on the soul of a receptive human. I have already shared the quite different impacts on me of two very disparate God-Beings: Isis and Sekhmet. Let's look in passing at the Isis Archetype: the nurturing mother, Goddess of Children, and devoted spouse of Osiris. Yet another example of a different Divine Presence is projected by the archetype of Athena, a Being of wise gravity, reason, and intellect, among other characteristics.

Because Divinity comes to us in the forms we understand, God-Beings appear to each of us in unique ways. The Source sends us the Divine Energy that we are capable of experiencing. Although you may never perceive Sekhmet, you can experience your own Source Being. That revelation may be one of the reasons you picked up this book or ordered it off the Internet. Whether we perceive a sacred event or not depends on what each of us is able or primed to see. Suggestions for developing your own spiritual receptivity abound throughout this book.

Sekhmet's archetype is complex and contradictory, as I have already suggested. (So is Jehovah.) The Roamer of the Desert, She is also the Lady of the Lake, the sacred body of water at Karnak. In the latter guise, She represents the fertility of lands and people, rebirth, purification, and renewal. Just as She carries radiant Light, She also carries darkness. She is the Destroyer, the Lady of Plague and Pestilence, the Goddess of War, the Terrible One. Yet She is simultaneously the compassionate healer Who transforms the world and our consciousness.

Like many Fire Goddesses, she is passionate, energetic, and fierce. Just as renewal and re-creation emerge from the ashes of fire, She is a Creator (perhaps one of the seven creative rays that beam from the Source in some ancient creation myths), referred to in some references as the "primal and Supreme creative Power."

Awareness of Deity

Knowing the Sacred, knowing Sekhmet, means understanding Her historical significance. Possibly one of the most ancient of God-Spirits (as you already know), She existed—and was adoringly worshipped—thousands of years before the Old Testament was written. Dr. Robert Masters, after a scholarly lifetime studying Her, refers to Her in *The Goddess Sekhmet* as "the oldest Deity known to the human race, along with Set." He goes on to explain: "Set is the Urgod of Chaos and the principal antagonist of Sekhmet in the War in Heaven." Bob then adds:

> *... it is not really possible to say which of these Gods preceded the other or whether perhaps they came to be in simultaneity. That they are the oldest Deities—and Beings—is generally accepted in the Egyptian, as well as many other, spiritual, magical, and occult Traditions.*

As I say, the presence of any Sacred Being is complicated, and devotion to Spirit is neither simple nor easy. Sekhmet is not known as the Lady of Change and Transformation without good cause! Yet She is sublime beyond measure, and loving us flawed humans is Her unparalleled joy.

Magnetic Force

I have spoken earlier of Sekhmet's magnetic energy. Her Divine Force attracted people, events, and even animals to me to assist my Journey. Bob Masters was one of those individuals. His psycho-spiritual energy was complex, often uneven. In my mind, I thought of him as a kind of Teddy Roosevelt, a spiritual Rough Rider. Sturdy, blunt, and metaphysically curious, he was absolutely Sekhmet's choice as my Neter. I, who was still a bred-in-the-bone academic, had yet to learn the practices (meditation, dance, yoga, and so on) for living fully in my body, rituals essential to access and enlarge the body-mind-spirit fusion. Bob's energy challenged mine; his intellect continuously paced me at a fast clip; and his directness cut through my façades.

How does this discussion of the Goddess's purview matter? Because it again reminds us of how Divine omnipotence, omniscience, and omnipresence permeate the past and the present, all that is and has ever been. The much-touted contemporary search for the "God Gene" presumes that a specific gene in each of us predisposes us to spiritual experiences. Some scientists now suggest the possibility that faith is a product of biology, which may well have triggered human religious behavior and rituals that go as far back as hunter-gatherers in 7,000 BC (according to Wade Nicholas writing in the *New York Times,* November 14, 2009). The speculation—and perhaps the proof—of such thinking provides evidence throughout human history of the names of many Deities. In my mind, the names do not matter as much as the fact that there exists a long history of human faith in a Divine Force.

Even more to the point, however, is the possibility that we are, indeed, hardwired to have mystical experiences of Spirit. There have been times in history, I believe, when revelatory events were not uncommon, when people communicated directly with Divine Beings, when this reality was interwoven in our daily lives. The history of the Mystical Tradition is rich with stories and evidence of this contact. Myths, sacred writings, rituals, saints, magic, and healing Wicca or shamans were alive in the reality paradigms. Perhaps, then, it was possible for individuals to speak with Spirit without the interference that now obstructs the flow of our hearts. Yet the mystical impulse still exists within each of us, as Sekhmet's story suggests. For me, the Sacred Dreams and Her words are proof of Divine Being, just as you will discover evidence for your own sacred Knowledge.

Synchronicity

As I was revising this chapter, I continued to face a writer's dilemma described previously. The bare bones of that dilemma are this: How do you describe the ineffable? How can I convey Sekhmet's magnetic force to you without using language that might seem overblown? Her presence at Karnak, as well as since then, was so transcendent that it requires an intensity of descriptors to recreate it for your understanding.

My desire is that you understand the vibratory experience without being turned off by my lavish language.

As I struggled with this, I turned the TV on to Oprah's *Super Soul Sunday*, without knowing who her guest might be. On that Sunday morning it was, with perfect synchronicity, Dr. Eben Alexander. His bestselling book, *Proof of Heaven*, is his narration of a Divine experience very much like my own. Although his was a near-death occurrence (he spent seven days in a coma), he and I were similarly transported by parallel experiences of infinite love and overwhelming awe. In the interview with Oprah (May 12, 2013, OWN Network), he uses the same vocabulary I do in this narrative, speaking of a Divine Being (whom he calls "Om") as "awesome beyond anything I could imagine." He describes a perception of "infinite space and all eternity," as he was immersed in the "power and love of that all loving, infinitely Divine." As the interview continued, he gave words to our similar experience of Ego Annihilation, stating, "This was not Eben Alexander's consciousness; it was All Consciousness." The commonality of our experiences was drawn together when he told Oprah his first words when he came out of his seven-day coma: "All is well."

Listening to him describe his experience of being in the Presence of the Living God, I resonated to his choice of words. Although his language may seem over the top to a reader or listener, to me it was a reassuring validation of precisely what I had felt and known at Karnak. He and I echoed each other's descriptive language; after all, we had each witnessed similar profound spiritual realities. Dr. Alexander speaks the words of my own heart when he says, "You can spend the rest of your life and you'll never know all the meaning of this."

Reflections: Chapter Nine

Most of us feel belief, doubt, skepticism, atheistic denial—as well as combinations of all these—as our lives evolve. Reflections for this chapter are deliberately open-ended to encourage your own thoughts about doubt and belief.

1. Writing in your journal, describe where you are now in your belief—or lack thereof—in the Divine; use all the vocabulary words fitting your psychic situation.
2. How would you define the Mysteries or Mysticism?
3. What are the critical events now influencing your faith or belief system?
4. Do you resent these questions, or do you welcome this intellectual probing? In either case—why?

CHAPTER TEN

Initiation into Sacred Dreams

There is an aura of enchantment around our dreams. Even nightmares have a potent mystique. They are real—and yet they are not. We are submerged in the unconscious, in a kind of trance condition. Although Lucid Dreaming may grant us some control over the images and visions, the machinery of how dreams work and the reasons why we dream are still mysterious. Are dreams simply a projection of our unconscious minds? Or do they embody different dimensions of reality? In my own case with the Sacred Dreaming Time, I was taken over by a different dream experience that doesn't fit any of the typical categories.

Histories and biographies are abundant with true dream experiences—from the numerous prophetic dreams in the Bible to modern research into Lucid Dreaming. Yet the meaning of our dreams remains, for the most part, enigmatic, that ninety percent of the iceberg still lurking beneath the waters of the unconscious. Do supernatural dream scenarios designate portals opening to the Divine? Are we merely descending into our anxieties playing out through dream scenarios? Are dreams pathways to other realities? As you read the unfolding dreams sent by Sekhmet, you will make your own judgments about their meanings and messages, including the otherworld realities conveyed within them. I share them with you as my own esoteric experiences and as a compelling narrative within this broader narrative about enlarging consciousness.

Rituals of Lucid Dreaming did not work for me, because Sekhmet's energy immersed me immediately; she drew me into a dream vortex in which I was powerless to do anything but experience and absorb the dreams. In this state, time and space did not exist. She had purpose and intent with the dreams, and I was Her student/priestess/daughter receiving Her gift. In the accumulations of my dream messages, I could interpret each separate nightly image, but that was not Her purpose. The significance of Sekhmet's "directed dreams" was like an orchestra conductor directing our attention to themes of the entire symphony (not simply the individual motifs). In a similar fashion, my dreams possessed shape (as I mentioned earlier) like the structure of a symphony, with recurrent themes or patterns. Over the ten-month period, my dreams evolved from mini-lessons to purposive messages from the God/dess, in the same way as my spiritual consciousness evolved. As the dream saga was revealed, the boundaries between What Is Known and What Is Unknown grew more transparent.

At that point, the dreams also became interactive, rather than passive. Sekhmet now had expectations of me to put the puzzle pieces in place, to determine—stretching my intelligent imagination—not only the immediate meaning, but the definition of a larger truth. My role was not simply to receive the nightly tales, but to process, synthesize, understand, and disseminate metaphysical information. In acknowledging that role, I became an active seeker, the Hierophant for whom teaching and learning are Divine acts, evocative with purpose.

Panoply of Dreams

Although there are many paths to Sekhmet, She seems to favor dreams as especially effective. Recall that in *The Goddess Sekhmet* Dr. Masters speaks of dreams as a link to Sekhmet, as well as Her preferred manner of communicating with us. From the beginning of Her recognized existence (more than 5,000 years ago), She has sent Her dreams to us. Over eons, human beings have invited Her wisdom by various rituals to prepare for Her presence in dreams. Even today, some of us who have incomparable encounters with Her often experience those through Her evocative dreams, and She continues to send me messages through dreams (as well as other means).

Normandi Ellis, the Egyptian scholar previously cited, affirms Sekhmet's communication with us when our sleeping minds are in a different state of awareness; we have slipped into another dimension (perhaps more than one). She and I each believe that dream states can be called forth, although they may also appear spontaneously. In either case, Sekhmet's presence is central. Ellis refers to the ancient Ebers Medical Papyrus as evidence that dream spells existed in ancient Egypt, including "several dream spells that invoke the Goddess Sekhmet." Clearly, the practice of calling Her presence and dreams through rituals was not uncommon thousands of years ago. It is yet within our power to use dreaming as a tool to summon Her awesome presence. Although that power still exists, it is our ritual memory that has faded—and even that can be recalled, invoked through various words and symbolic actions. What the ancient mystics, temple priest/ esses, shamans understood can—through rites, recovered language, visualizations, and dream lore—be recalled to our consciousness, their effectiveness intact.

Into the Deep of Teaching Dreams

The ten and one-half month span of my Dreaming Time is remarkable, but it is not singularly unique; prolonged dreaming over months, perhaps over years, has occurred with other God-Beings who communicated so profoundly with humans (Pallas Athena, Isis, and Odin, for example). The history of mystical dreams is fragmentary, even in documenting the experiences of contemporary dreamers. There may be many reasons for the lack of consistent contemporary information: fear, self-doubt, confusion about what the dreams mean and why they have occurred, and the existence of few acceptable research platforms for open discussion. The expansion of social media may offer us opportunities for sharing dream experiences, but there is a Wild West flavor to some digital communication, especially with esoteric topics.

Nevertheless, there remain overlapping commonalities in recorded mystical dream experiences from thousands of years ago to the twenty-first century:

- They are intense;
- They have meaning or guiding messages (often commands from spiritual forces);
- They are outside of time and geography;
- They are centered on the appearance of a powerful Spiritual Entity that evokes fascination and awe—and sometimes fear;
- They are spontaneous, although dreams may also be invoked by rituals.

These observations, of course, echo William James's summary of mystical characteristics in general, but I repeat them as a reminder that I am discussing *mystical* dreams. Although Mysticism may be referred to separately from dreams, mystical dreams are part of the larger subject.

Whenever I closed my eyes at night or during brief naps, the dreams would start. Because I kept my notes after every dream, I recall exactly what happened as I spent months immersed in Her Presence. When I awoke from a dream, I scrambled to reach my journal, and I recorded the prime memory with eagerness, curiosity, and anticipation. Accounts of the dreams, written immediately upon waking, are the evidence I have for the intensity of spiritual contact with Sekhmet, as well as the apparent organization of information She presented; but it is, I am convinced, extraordinary and compelling evidence.

The dream journals I meticulously kept served as a fundamental resource for this narrative, assuring me that the recorded details were genuine accounts then—and that they remain so today. Additionally, my journal record allows me to continue decoding the answers to crucial questions raised by the scenarios: What did I understand at the time of the initial dreams, and what do I better understand about these events twenty years later? Of course, the perceptions are deeper now, the result of additional decades of lived experiences and communication with the Goddess. The dreams have not changed, but my insights have evolved. This is also a critical insight about the importance of your dream journals. They matter at the time of writing down the scenarios because the remembered details are still vivid. Equally important, you have a reference point to which you can return; you have evidence of the dream events. Since the significance of sacred dreams is intensified as time passes, the events take on the enrichment of your life knowledge. You will know when one or more of your dreams presents supernatural realities; and you will also be alert to the uniqueness of contiguous dreaming with clustered messages. Don't let these dreams slip away. Acknowledge, explore them, discover their meanings for your life and spiritual journey. Esoteric dreams matter only to the extent that each of us takes note of them. As pointed out earlier, Awareness is an essential tool for cross-dimensional consciousness.

Let me repeat a salient point already stated. On rare occasions when neither Bob nor I could interpret the meaning of a dream, he would say, "Read over your journals again; look for the whole picture. Always look for patterns. Eventually, some meanings will emerge that aren't apparent now. Remember, these are teaching dreams; She expects you to gain an accumulation of meaning over time." These are the same words I am speaking to you now.

Metaphorical Baptism

Early in December 1996, after months of enthralling dreaming (described in detail in the following chapters), the dreams began to dwindle in occurrence. They diminished to three times a week; eventually they appeared only once a week, until finally the intense frequency ended. I was bereft—I felt as if my heart had died. Although I did not understand why so much rapture was now gone from my daily life, Sekhmet let me know that it was merely part of the process. That is my language, not Hers, but Her meaning was crisp: *the Dream Time has served its purpose, and you and I are moving on.* I thought She meant moving in different directions, rather than together. However, that is not at all what She intended. When She claimed me, She meant there would always be a Divine link between us, and I would be Her *avatar* as long as I drew breath.

During a December visit that year with Bob Masters and Jean Houston, I asked Jean, "Why have the dreams stopped? I am filled with grief. Have I done something wrong? Is Sekhmet offended? Is She abandoning me?"

After asking what Sekhmet Herself had explained to me, Jean said, "As Sekhmet has told you, the dreams have accomplished their purposes. You don't need the dreaming time any more. Sekhmet doesn't have to communicate with you by dreaming. She has prepared you, rewired you to deal with Her directly. Ask Her how She wants to come to you now."

That conversation provided comfort and information. Sekhmet did show me a cosmic place (as I have already described) where I now encounter Her routinely to receive Her counsel. Of course, Sekhmet is ubiquitous. But I have learned that imagining an otherworldly, or worldly, locus is a tool allowing me to encounter Her more easily, even when I get buried in my own stuff.

Nevertheless, in the midst of this activity, Sekhmet continued to deliver spiritual insights, many of which I am sharing with you throughout this book. This is one of the intuitive understandings I have found to be true about psycho-spiritual experiences. When you are the recipient of a significant esoteric happening, the event itself is only a small portion of its importance. What Bob and Jean both taught me is that *process* is crucial to the follow-through. No matter how delicious the experience, or how often Divine appearances occur, they are transient. A crucial part of the process of unveiling the meaning is the reflection we engage in afterward. At that point, we can ask ourselves the provocative questions and attempt to synthesize information. The written record in our journals allow us to revisit these events as often as needed. Our contemplation of spiritual experiences after the fact, for which unencumbered time is required, allows us gradually to peel the onion of interpretation. Above all, to the best of our ability, we must ensure that nothing will be lost of Divine communication.

Equally important is our need for wise and knowledgeable colleagues with whom to talk. So many of our perceived ideas must be tested through dialogue with other scholars, teachers, and seekers, as well as our continued dreaming. One of my challenges was creating a network of trusted metaphysicians, shamans, mystics. To find even one person who possessed all these traits and was, at the same time, down-to-earth, was a challenge, as it may be for you, too.

Bob once said to me that learning *discernment* was one of the most salient outcomes of a metaphysical event. The ability to distinguish the authentic from the faux, and the true event from the illusion, is a spiritual discipline much sought after and difficult to master. Developing such insights occurs only when we have passed through a personal initiation that requires a complete sensate and psychic experience, such as the one I described at Karnak. (The Dreaming Time continued that spiritual initiation.) This is a metaphorical immersion, baptism, sacred rite.

Reflections: Chapter Ten

Spiritual beings are everywhere manifest in our lives. In our culture, however, we do not have a consistent context for acknowledging or understanding their presence. We are, at best, skeptical of various kinds of spirit communication and, at worst, afraid. Because we are seldom trained to listen to or perceive these realities, let's take a look at that belief structure, with all possibilities in mind to modify or replace some of those beliefs. (Do you understand how the action of writing in your journal clarifies your thinking?)

1. What is the single most important cultural belief you hold that inhibits your ability to be open to a wide range of spiritual communication?
2. If you already possess a mind open to metaphysical possibilities, write down in your journal the two or three most meaningful principles of your own Possibility thinking.
3. If you have difficulty expanding the edges of your belief system, write down what you could dare to believe if you took *fear* or *self-judgment* out of the equation.

4. Is reading this book opening up challenges to you? What are those challenges, and does the narrative help you deal with them?

If, as you are journaling, you find that the writing is difficult, I recommend a first-rate book on the writing process: Julia Cameron's *The Artist's Way.*

CHAPTER ELEVEN

Dreams as Divine Communication

We travel beyond safe, comfortable thinking as we journey into the esoteric, the invisible world of ambient uncertainty where our path lies. However, this is also where our greatest metaphysical challenges lurk, those with shadowy outlines not clearly defined. In this context, Sacred Dreams and other mysterious events help reveal their meaning. What we believe is possible becomes Possible—through our intentional thoughts, as the latest quantum physics suggests. By moving the boundaries of our belief systems, we can authentically comprehend Sacred Dreaming, for example, as a spiritual process and a channel for the most profound Divine connections.

Since dreams were my most compelling communication route with Sekhmet, and since they consumed almost a year of my life and continue today, let's spend more time on that topic. The dreaming experiences transformed my beliefs and every aspect of my life. But the story of my dreams, as I emphasize repeatedly, is not the tale of me, Helena. It is, rather, the narrative of dream consciousness for each of us, of touching that consciousness and then using its power to teach this transformation to one another. Each of us dreams, each of us thinks about the meanings of those dreams, each of us has met and been guided by Divine Beings in our dream fields. Dreaming, an aspect of universal consciousness, is a bond that links our human and all sensate communities together.

Dreams are strange, elusive entities, but we can learn to control both their content and their stabilization (that is, our ability to hold a dream while prolonging its duration). My desire is that you are drawn to understand the nature of my narrative, see your own consciousness mirrored in the descriptions of others' consciousness, and bring your passion to the universal themes of spiritual self-discovery. To achieve that, you may want to know how to effect dream consciousness on your own. The dreams I will share in some detail a few pages farther on are not just my private dreams filled with quests, Sacred Beings, "receptive consciousness," Enlightenment, the Hero/ine's Journey, and so on. Repeating an observation made earlier: These dreams and themes do not belong to me alone; they are the sacred messages and possibilities inherent in dreaming for each of us.

To return to the point: How do I do this myself? Lucid Dreaming is where we will start. Defining the term is easy: "awake dreaming," "being conscious during your dreams," "being aware that you are dreaming and having control over that process." Although some references give up to fifty-two tips for practicing Lucid Dreaming, I am going to suggest that the following easy steps will serve you well:

- Keep a dream journal to track your dreams, steps followed, and outcomes; this is also a reality check about dream content.
- Before sleep, prepare yourself for dreaming: pray, meditate (if that is your practice at night), adjust your emotions for composure, consciously set aside the business of the day, and get comfortable in your bed or couch.
- Visualize what you wish to dream about, what information you are requesting; set your intent.
- Find triggers that cue you for conscious dreaming as opposed to regular sleep. Triggers can be words, phrases, symbols, images, whatever causes your brain to recognize that Lucid Dreaming is underway.
- Repeat your signal affirmations.
- After 4½ to 6 hours of sleep, train your consciousness to wake up; repeat your intent, and then go back to sleep. Your brain will be newly alert while your body will be set for more sleep. Both levels of consciousness are then in play, and research shows that you are more likely to experience conscious dreaming.

- Write the results in your Dream Journal immediately. Do not go to the bathroom, do not stop for a cup of coffee, and do not talk to anyone. Go to your journal first.

You may not be able to effect Lucid Dreaming every time you attempt it, but the more often you follow these guidelines, the more proficient you will become. At the end of this book I have cited websites that will be helpful if you decide to pursue Lucid Dreaming.

My own dreaming technique was similar:

- Keep your dream journal and pen beside your bed or sleeping area.
- Take four to five minutes in prayer or meditation to set a tone of love and gratitude in your mind.
- Set your intention, and state it aloud as a kind of mantra. Mine was always to be receptive to Sekhmet's dreams, to remember them, and to foster serial dreaming.
- Place your hands on your heart. Even if you sleep on your side or stomach, cross your hands over your heart for 30 seconds or so.
- Go into your sleeping position prepared to fall asleep at once. My mantra is *Sa Sekhem Sahu,* meaning, "The Breath of Life, the Might, the Realized Human."

The simplicity of this process reinforces our earlier discussions of Awareness, Attention, and so on in Chapter 4.

For nearly a year, Sekhmet brought hundreds of sacred dreams to me every time I closed my eyes to sleep or nap. The nightly visions sparkled, dazzled, exploded, and *swooshed* through my unconscious mind. There was urgency to the frequency—as if the Goddess had so much to show me that every dream moment had to be filled with revelations. The dreams were also alive with sensory images—brilliant colors, sounds and dialogue, kinesthetic sensations, and so on. The vitality did not merely involve my physical self, but the "subtle body" or invisible energetic essences surrounding each of us, as well.

Process of Dream Ritual

The elements of ritual create a sense of remarkable connection between the dreamer and the Sacred One. Because these dream experiences were rare and unique, I refer to them simply as "Sacred Dreaming." Even that phrase does not adequately define the conscious creation of dreams that play out in the unconscious. My experience is set apart from many other dream events by the long, continuous time span of the sleep visions (ten and one-half months), as well as by the progressive meaning of the dreams (as you will see). The dreams tell a story as they unfold. Meaning builds upon meaning in the sequences to create a mythic narrative as the dreams continued.

Sekhmet's intent—which at first I did not absorb—was clear almost immediately. Divine Intentionality may be as much a key to interpreting the dream content as is our own stated intention. As She swept me up, I entered another dimension of the psyche. The discipline required to observe fully and then record every detail immediately afterwards was demanding—"time sensitive," as we say about urgent matters. Dreams, even those rife with details, are memory phantoms; they disappear before they can be completely written down.

Definitive patterns emerged soon after the dreams began. Neither the dreams nor the patterns were random or hit-and-miss. As is clear from the characteristics of the Dream Ritual outlined below, Sekhmet had strong intent in sending the dreams. They were another aspect of Her claiming me.

- The dreams occurred every day, sometimes three or four times a day.
- They frequently were presented in the compact intensity of parables.
- They usually concluded with Sekhmet bringing me back to consciousness with these words: "Wake up and record this dream." In the moments of first awakening, I have often seen Her shadowy figure either beside, or at the foot of, my bed.

- The dreams were expressed in exaggerated colors, like early Technicolor movies, vivid colors that heightened the drama.
- Most of the dreams involved simply Sekhmet and me.
- Generally, the dreams took place against a vast and luminous, blue-black ether, beyond the markers of time and space.
- Although Sekhmet generally communicates with me through concepts projected from Her mind to mine, She occasionally speaks to me in words and sentences in the dreams.
- In many dreams, She showcases Her strong lion head in different poses (full, half, three-quarters), representing varied emotional states (maternal, fiery, compassionate, infinitely loving). In doing so, She also emphasizes that we must not be deterred by Her fierce head. In one of Her "Lion" dreams (September 20, 1997), She pronounces, "Hear me. 'Lion' is not word enough for Me. 'Lion' does not hold Me. Know what I am."
- Often the Goddess rapidly shifts Her bodily movements—standing, striding, dancing, and sitting—in different dress, with burning colors (usually red or gold). I believe She is showing Her numerous Divine aspects, displaying the complexity of Her Being.
- She brought me dreams by "request" (I hesitate to say "on demand" when referring to Sekhmet). I would pose a metaphysical question to Her, fall asleep, and the dream answer would be immediate, as the reader will see in the ensuing descriptions.
- Many times after awakening I told Her that I did not get all of Her message, or I couldn't remember all of the dream narrative. She would tell me to go back to sleep and—although it sounds incredible—rerun the dream for me, like striking the playback button on the DVR.
- Usually, dreams would be sequential; occasionally a dream would be continued (episodes one, two, and three—not to be irreverent, but like a TV series) over several nights, even while new dreams also occurred in between. This is true of the three Kwan Yin segments described later.
- The purpose of the dreaming is to impart information to me, not to give psychic prophecies (although on rare occasions,

She does foreshadow). The graphic images of Sekhmet in the war-torn landscape, which I will describe later, are examples of a glimpse into the future.

- The dreams took me through the classic steps of the Hero/ine's Journey (discussed in Chapter 12). Because those steps provide the mythic framework for understanding thematic dreams at deeper levels, they deserve a longer discussion. The dreams—as I comprehend them—simultaneously led me through a mystic initiation into the lessons of the ancient Egyptian Mystery Schools (see Chapter 5, "Mystery of Mysteries"), as well as the Hero/ine's Journey toward Enlightenment.

Impact of the Dreams

When I recently read these characteristics aloud to a writing class I was taking, there were many questions from the group.

The professor was the first to comment. "This must have been exhausting! Did you ever ask Her to give you a breather?"

Members of the group chuckled, and so did I. I never thought about slowing things down; I was too enthralled by nightly parables and communication with my Beloved Sekhmet to question the pace.

"No," I said, "I was just stunned by what was happening—and so humbled—that I accepted events as they happened. Besides that, how—really—do you ask a Goddess to slow down?"

"How did you run your daily life?" a classmate from Estonia asked. "How was there time to think about anything else?"

"Good question." I mulled that over for a moment. "The truth is, I was enveloped in an amazing energy that simply carried me along. And I was enchanted. Under a spell. I wouldn't have given up one moment of these magical events. Maybe it would be helpful to you if I described it this way: the experience was not unlike those first emotions when you are on the brink of a spectacular, all-consuming love. The passion just overtakes you!"

"Tell us more details about your feelings about the experience," a classmate requested. "I want to know more about what you *felt* as it happened—and afterwards. And now that you've had years to decode the dreams, how do you feel? Do you really have a better understanding of what they mean?"

"You know, it's a lifelong search for meaning. It truly is a process. Many of the dreams were 'quick reads.' But there are still a few Sekhmet dreams I haven't yet deciphered to my satisfaction."

"I am bothered by something else," our professor commented. "Our dreams help us work through fears and anxieties; they're necessary for mental health. Did you have other, more mundane dreams at the same time?"

"Hmmm," I hadn't thought about that before. Looking back on those months, I wasn't sure. "In my dream journal, I recorded only the Sekhmet dreams, and they are the only occurrences I remember. If much other dreaming went on, it didn't seem important at the time."

For some of my colleagues and classmates, these descriptions seemed weird. Acknowledging that fact is important. Revelatory events, however enticing they are, are also uncanny. And they are happening with greater frequency to more of us. You could be the one next time, standing in front of a group to explain the Mysteries as you have experienced them.

"These dreams were not those we ordinarily receive," I continued my response to the class. "They were immersive—all-consuming, message-driven, and like an extended baptism into New Being. These events are ineffable—they defy description. I can't tell you more than that."

Responses from class members—fascinated, cautious, curious, freaked out—were invaluable in providing critical insights for me as a writer, especially as I learned that people want to know about the *emotions* involved in paranormal experiences. I had a tendency, for example, to describe the rational outlines of an event, but neglect to address the messier issues of the heart. Individuals in the class sought to understand not only what happened in the dream, but—far more important to them—how did these events make me feel? Only after that could they ask the greater question: What does this mean to each one of us? Is your takeaway similar to what mine would be? Now I ask the reader: How do these questions resonate with you right now?

The class's reactions also helped me understand myself as a narrator. My conviction in what I had experienced and what I knew had to be firm; without that confidence in these realities, pieces of me would have crumbled. Presenting my dreams is, as I believe Sekhmet intends, not merely describing curious metaphysical events, but a metaphysical challenge about thought transformation for each of us in the world. The dreams were not ordinary occurrences, and they summoned me—and possibly you, too—to a transformative purpose.

Preparing for Sacred Immersion

When I returned to the Dream Journals three years ago to select passages for sharing in this narrative, I was again struck by the abundance of Sekhmet's gift.

Did Sekhmet give me an introduction to the dream process? Did She provide special preparation for me to receive Her teachings? Of course not! I felt as if She simply flung me into this cross-dimensional reality without a content index. Although Sekhmet's presence is compassionate, She also sometimes uses the "sink or swim" approach to esoteric learning. Such was the case with the dream experiences. Part of my paranormal education under Sekhmet's tutelage was to manage paradoxes, solve esoteric puzzles, and find my inner gyroscope while living upended in the Mysteries. That behavior, as I and other followers have experienced, is Her typical modus operandi.

Early in the dream occurrences, Bob introduced me to complementary processes: past life regressions, automatic writing, and deep trance meditation, each of them essential psycho-spiritual tools for the Sekhmet work. I needed to learn how to receive and process Her information on Her terms. I realized we were speaking an ancient metaphysical language with an almost entirely new vocabulary. It was a language made for esoteric transits between the conscious and unconscious mind, dreaming and awake.

Because of the complexity of that time, I have struggled to find the most effective way to present these dreams to you. It makes sense, for clarity's sake, simply to group the dreams into four clusters, as outlined below. Rereading, reviewing, and meditating on these dreams have revealed what appears to be an intentional order in Sekhmet's scenarios. As I stated before, I am not speaking of Lucid Dreaming; I am describing an energetic phenomenon engulfing every aspect of my being for almost a year. She transported and immersed me in a cosmic consciousness that I will never be able to interpret fully; it is beyond human *knowing*. She took me, and continues to take me, into profound Mysteries. It is possible that each of us could make similar journeys if we would allow our minds to encompass the expanded metaphysical possibilities that do exist.

For clarity now, I have grouped the dreams as follows:

- **Introduction and Play**—These early dreams present—for lack of a better phrase—an elementary, metaphysical curriculum. As you will see, Sekhmet and Bob (as guiding presences) demonstrate principles of time/no time and simplified quantum physics. In addition, comic dreams occur, such as the whimsical dream in which She and Bob are lifting off the top of my head to pour in knowledge. (Such scenarios remind us that Divine Spirits have a sense of humor.) Do not be surprised if some of your mystical experiences are funny. We sometimes forget that revelations come in many forms, including jokes, as do the Supreme Beings who bring them to us. (Think of the fanciful depictions of the Hindu Elephant God Ganesha.)
- **Sacred Energy**—Some of the dreams are what I call Sacred Energy Dreams. In these, Sekhmet dances, demonstrating repeatedly how She *is* the energy of life. "I am here! I am alive!" She declares. Not a dream figure, She asserts Her presence as a Divine Being in full vitality.

Both the Introduction and Sacred Energy Dreams are initiatory, demonstrating some of the knowledge and characteristics needed in the quest to come. She reiterates basic spiritual tools shown in the dreams, such as the capacity to love, devotion to Spirit, power of mind, concentrated focus, freedom to think beyond cultural concepts of time and place, understanding the nature of universal energy, developing the power of manifestation, among others. In this way, She defines the qualities of expanding consciousness. Surprisingly, She even engaged in a kind of wooing in the dreams, a seduction of my spirit, not unlike a lover enticing the beloved. It is a given, of course, that Divine Source does not need to please, woo, or show off for us; generally, it's the other way around as we seek to display our devotion to the Sacred Entity. Yet the unconditional love given by Sekhmet is the same love emanating from all Sacred Beings: Divine love without judgment and with complete acceptance of our humanity. Sekhmet's radiant displays in the dreams were Her exuberant, energetic expressions of this love.

- **Quest or Journey**—This third dream category, more complex and parabolic than the earlier scenarios, encompasses the majority of the dreams. The sequencing in the third stage led me from simple to more difficult knowledge. These were dreams granted after I had completed the initial dream sequences and was now ready for the demands of my deepened spiritual quest. The later dreams, then, also became a metaphorical guide to the experience and trials of the Hero/ine's Journey. To meet each symbolic test successfully is to move through all levels of knowing and esoteric skill, confronting graduated difficulties, until the Journey's completion.

- **Foreshadowing**—A fourth dream pattern also occurred, out of sequence and haunting in its ancient and contemporary meaning. Essentially the same dream recurred several times during a fifteen-month period in the midst of the other dreams: sporadic *dreaming interruptus*. Unlike Her typical dream colors, these dreams are in shades of gray and black. The template is the same for each of them: Sekhmet is walking, grief-stricken, across a war-torn landscape, the expression on Her face as ruined as the devastated land. This dream sequence, presenting Her rare prophesies, occurred years before our country's incursions into the Middle East. As a healer and protector of humankind, in 1995-97, Sekhmet foreshadows the endless wars soon to come.

The dream scenarios, as I have already suggested, were laid out like a school curriculum extending from spiritual kindergarten (simple esoteric concepts in the earliest dreams), to eventual passage through the Final Gate of metaphysical understanding at the end of the journey. As is true of all spiritual quests, the goal is to attain consciousness of All Knowing, while still understanding that the core of esoteric knowledge remains Unknowable. Only part of the veil may be lifted during mortal life. Still, spiritual Hero/ines as we are, we are challenged to complete the difficult quest.

Sharing these dreams with you has significance beyond describing a cool personal experience. This narrative is about me and my connection with the Great Lady, but it is also a sweeping revelation by a Goddess of the vastness of All That Is. Our Divine invitation to recognize esoteric matters far beyond ourselves is also a summons to understand that the individual experiences of each of us connects to greater Sacred purposes.

This, as I understand it from the Dreaming Time, is our Sacred Call:

- To *know*
- To *understand*
- To *act* in the world

Reflections: Chapter Eleven

Keeping a Dream Journal, along with other daily reflections, can be sources for the revelation of infinite esoteric possibilities.

115

1. Whether or not you keep a special journal for dreams, as you think about your most significant dreams over the years, do you perceive any patterns, recurrent themes, or repeated scenarios?
2. What insights about yourself and your esoteric life come from your dreams?
3. Have you attempted Lucid Dreaming techniques before? Whether or not you have, consider trying for yourself the techniques outlined in this chapter. It may take a week or more to establish the ritual, so allow yourself the time required.
4. Did the techniques work for you? Make notes about whether the techniques were successful or not.
5. What themes and observations in this chapter are especially insightful for you?
6. How might you use those insights in your own journey?

CHAPTER TWELVE

Consciousness Awakens

The Dreaming Time has, like a partially translated hieroglyph, intrigued me for years. The dream design, more obvious to me now, has always been present, of course, but I needed time and distance to see it. On the surface, the dreams present, among other spiritual messages, a template of the mythic Hero/ine's Journey toward Enlightenment and Self-Knowledge (as I will discuss in the next chapter). However, many of the symbols and metaphorical interpretations are still subterranean, and these meanings will emerge in bits and pieces for the remainder of my life. One of the numerous gifts of writing this book has been the accumulated understanding of previously obscured meanings. To emphasize one more time: The dreams are not random metaphysical messages, I am convinced, but the instructive parables of Divine Intelligence.

Episodes from the Dreams

What follows are verbatim journal entries, dated and recorded (along with time of day or night) at the time of each dream. Because these are transcriptions written at the moment, the style is at times unpolished. I chose, however, to share each passage in the fresh immediacy of my first recollections. Only a fraction of the dreams are given here. To maintain the focus of this narrative, I have selected only those that continue moving the narrative along, summarizing longer dreams, and omitting the majority of them in these summaries. The dreams omitted are not shared because some of them are repetitive scenarios, or are too long to be effectively included. This narrative's purpose is to share with you a glimpse into the Unknown revealed by the dreams and to maintain narrative clarity.

To keep the dreams in a comprehensible time frame, let me repeat: The experience of the Dreaming Time took place over a ten and one-half month period, beginning sporadically even before I left Egypt. Although intense, often contiguous, dreams occupied a significant area of my unconscious mind during these months, at the same time the dreams left me highly energized in my waking life. I started a new business, worked with clients, wrote and published professional articles, frequently travelled for my work, and studied with Bob and Jean. It was as if the dreams channeled vitality into my conscious mind. Sacred, numinous energy also had to be flowing into my unconscious-ness for so many activities to be crowded into both my waking and dreaming hours.

As each of you undertake your own discovery of the Divine within, dreams will likely be aspects of your experience, worthy of your atten-tion. They are a fountainhead of vital information about the status of your spiritual story. *Pay attention*, as Sekhmet often says.

September 7, 1997 (Sharing the dreams with you begins several months into the Dreaming Time, after I started detailed journaling.)

Before sleep, I ask Sekhmet to explain the nature of reality. As the dream begins, the action unfolds from left to right as if we are moving across a stage. Both Sekhmet and Bob Masters, in his role of Neter, are present.

As the dream opens, Sekhmet shows me two thick, parallel, golden lines, about a yard apart. One line is chest high and the other is waist high.

"Bring these two lines together," She commands.

After a few moments of my deepest concentration, the lines have not moved, and I am exhausted from the physical and mental energy expended. "I can't do it," I say.

"Yes, you can," She responds firmly.

Bob enters the scene, and Sekhmet wordlessly communicates the situation. She nods at him.

Bob turns to me, "Focus. Concentrate. Concentrate on thinking the lines together."

As I once again project maximum effort, the two lines move slightly, closing the distance between them. Excited, I look at Bob.

"Good," he says. "Concentrate harder."

I pour my complete mental energy into the task, and slowly the lines move until they meet. Then they loop around each other in a thick, loose braid of the brightest gold. At this point, I recognize this is a simple quantum physics exercise, demonstrating the power of our thoughts to influence realities, moving quarks and atoms by the force of our minds.

"There. And that is how it is done," Bob states with satisfaction, concluding the episode. Sekhmet and Bob smile and nod at me, satisfied with this demonstration of mind power.

Although I was merely beginning to understand the energy of manifestation, Sekhmet used the dream to illustrate that all realities are malleable. Just as the golden lines in the dream merge through my mental power, so the force of the concentrated mind can change both the perception of reality and the reality itself. In other words, reality is an energetic illusion.

Sekhmet has answered my question.

When I wake up, I am still elated. Not only has a dream dialogue begun between the Goddess and me, but She is actively showing me how to use energy in manifestation, rather than merely to observe it passively. Because this dream opens with a seemingly impossible challenge, I understand by the conclusion of the dream that I have to shift my comprehension of what is possible, while also trusting the deeper powers of my mind (my unconscious); only then do I have the combined metaphysical resources to effect change. As the dream demonstrates, we can use the tools of transformation already discussed (visualizations and affirmations) with confidence in the capacities of our minds to respond.

September 22, 1997

Before falling asleep, I have been reading Michael Talbot's *The Holographic Universe*.

"Tell me about this, Sekhmet," I request as I put the book down, place my hands over my heart, and drift off to sleep.

Bob appears as the dream opens. "Let me tell you about Time," he says. He points to a black line that now appears at waist height. "This line is Time."

"No," I protest. "Time is not linear."

"Wait and watch," Bob replies. "I'll show you."

He follows the black line with his index finger, drawing it out for several feet, and then he begins rubbing it out with his hands. Next, he plunges his hands into a swirl of mist or smoke that rises as the black line disappears; he makes a motion as if he is trying to roll the mist into a ball. Impossible. As the mist gathers and disperses without form, he turns to me.

"This is the nature of Time—formless and ephemeral."

When I try to write down the dream upon waking, the details about the mist are not clear in my memory. As usual, I feel the presence of Sekhmet beside me.

"I didn't get it all, Sekhmet," I say. "Could you repeat the dream please?"

"Yes, Daughter," She responds gently. "Go back to sleep."

As She repeats the dream exactly, its meaning is clearer: time is only a construct (like the black line Bob erases) that does not exist in dimensional reality. All time is timeless. More than this, the images and constructs of all things are created by the human mind—just as Time is a construct.

Perceptions of infinity, dimensions, time, and space are frequently part of Sekhmet's teachings during the introductory dreams. Perceiving reality as an illusion grants me fresh intellectual and spiritual freedom, within and outside of my dreams. When Bob Masters erases the line of Time, I also grasp the infinite concept of Divine ubiquity. If Spirit is always everywhere, then theories of time and place are indeed irrelevant.

As She portrays the illusion of time, She also demonstrates the illusion of space or locus. In the Goddess's simultaneous appearances to selected individuals around the globe, sometimes in visions and often in dreams, She is omniscient and omnipresent, manifesting Her Divine Energy everywhere at once. Her presence is *awful* (inspiring reverential awe). Dreams *are* Sekhmet's channel to our human consciousness/ unconsciousness, regardless of our human fears. At the same time, the dreams reveal Her image or mask; we can see the animal face, but only as Her camouflage, without the fullness of Divine revelation. In our human state, we cannot see the Sacred Presence behind the lion head.

September 30, 1997

At one point in the Dreaming Time span, during an evening meditation, Sekhmet disclosed to me my Sacred Name, a secret designation known only to the recipient and to the God-Force Who gives it to us. By ancient tradition, that name can never be shared with anyone; even Bob Masters did not know it. A lyrical word, it is used when I invoke Her presence for spiritual rituals, to request healing or help for others, or express gratitude.

The power of naming is a significant act of creation. In sacred creation myths (including the Biblical story), God-Force creates the world by speaking it into being, by naming it vibrationally. Names are energy and meaning. To illustrate one aspect of this: our public names hold so much of our soul identity that speaking them aloud can call our spirits back into our bodies (as is sometimes the case with near-death experiences) or our unconscious into consciousness. How much more metaphysically powerful, then, is a hidden Sacred Name!

It may be that some of the esoteric concepts I share in this narrative do not appear relevant to you at this moment. But as you explore your own spiritual sensibilities, any paranormal experiences you may already have encountered (no matter how tentative you are about them) may already be imbedded in your psycho-spiritual reality. You may already know on some level of awareness, for example, your Sacred Name and what it means. As you imagine developing within yourself the "receptive consciousness" that invites an experience of the Mysteries, this knowledge will serve more profound esoteric purposes. The deeper your understanding of possibilities, the more you can absorb from the spiritual sources that surround you.

September 30, 1997

A full night of Sekhmet dreams, and a scintillating display of the Goddess! I wake up twice to write down descriptions. When I go back to sleep, the dreams continue exactly where they had left off, as if a pause button had been pushed, and then the play button resumed the story. Telling you about these additional links is part of showing you how affectionate and unique the dream process was. Sekhmet *attended* to every aspect.

In tonight's longest dream, Sekhmet appears sequentially in multiple forms: as the animated statue at Karnak, in Her Goddess form outlined with iridescent lights, and as a leaping lion. Throughout this display, I receive Her exuberant message: "I am here; I am real; I am dazzling; I am teaching you; you are my Daughter."

This Sekhmet is no distant Goddess, but a Divine Being enjoying the play of Her energy, aware of Her human audience. I, too, vibrate with Her love.

At the same time, I experience a new spiritual insight. In the dreams, Sekhmet is flooding my consciousness with spiritual revelations that acknowledge my ancient ties to Her. Such astonishing favor from Divine Energy is an unearned gift, yet She offered it generously. I understood, then, Her real message: *As I love you, Daughter, how can you not love yourself?* This same question is spiritually relevant for each of us. To understand the Mysteries of Spirit, each of us must *become* the lifelong practice of loving. If we are not courageous enough to confront our imperfect selves with compassionate love, we are stalled midway in the Journey. After transcribing a few more scenarios of dream content, it will make more sense to place self-love in a central context. Absolute love of self will then take on greater resonance as the Divine purpose that unifies our energy and Intent.

At the conclusion of this chapter, I will return again briefly to the topic of self-love, which is central to any discussion of developing consciousness. We yearn to love God Source, yet somehow we may forget that this is not possible without love for ourselves. After I've transcribed the sacred content of several more dreams, the significance of self-love will take its place in the panoply of our spiritual tools.

Returning to the Sacred Dreams

October 1, 1997

A summary of this lengthy dream follows:

The dream begins with a huge, holographic lion head, electric with authoritative, Divine energy. The impact of that golden head against a blue-black cosmic backdrop is hypnotic. No other objects are visible, and there is no action in the dream. At the dream's conclusion, Sekhmet tells me this dream emphasizes another view of Her God-Self in full power. She also reminds me to revere Her lion head, rather than find it distracting, for She is Sacred in whatever form She takes.

"Know me!" She commands.

Sekhmet seems to understand and accept my initial reluctance to revere a lion-headed Divinity. The form a Deity takes, however, is irrelevant if Spirit is present, as Sekhmet informs me. However the God of Many Masks is revealed as we journey, we are bound to honor and surrender to whichever Divinity we are called to serve.

October 11, 1997

Sometimes Sekhmet is playful in my dreams; the following dream shows one of those quirky episodes.

The dream begins with my disembodied, shaved head, four feet tall, resting on the desert sand. My eyes are moving and I am fully alert; my brain is alive, although my physical body has disappeared. Yet, simultaneously, I am also

123

completely intact, standing beside the head, observing the action, along with Bob and the Goddess.

Bob lifts off the top of my head. A small hinge at the back of the skull allows the top to be tilted back, like the lid of a hinged box, to expose my entire brain. Several times he playfully lifts up the top of my head, letting it drop back, lifting it up again, the action making a slight "plopping" sound. Around my head at the level of the third eye is a dotted line encircling the skull. On the dotted line, these words are written: "Fill me up."

Sekhmet and Bob chuckle; they are having such a good time! I, however, am chagrined that the two of them are behaving with such cavalier manners. After all, I have been seeking the Secrets of the Mysteries, not a cosmic comedy. Finally, they turn to me with great affection and tenderness, at which point the Goddess, gently chuckling, assures me that the process of filling up my brain with spiritual knowledge is already underway.

Embarrassed, I am once more reminded that the Universe does have a sense of humor.

There is not a moment of unkindness in the dream, just delight in the ridiculous.

As She often does at the conclusion of a dream or visit, Sekhmet repeats her mantra: "All is well."

October 13, 1997

Once again, a long dream is abbreviated for this narrative.

The dream opens as Bob appears in his Hierophant persona, garbed in royal blue robes. He is teaching me about archetypes and how to work with them. (I use the word "archetype" in this context to mean the symbolic persona of a Divine Being. Recall the warrior persona of Athena as She battled to save the City of Athens, or that of Artemis, the huntress with Her quiver of arrows, always accompanied by Her canine companions.)

In the dream, Bob speaks: "Archetypes are not humans writ large. They have their own way of doing things, within parameters that have nothing to do with this plane of existence."

(Twenty years later, as I am writing this book, I still hear Bob's words telling me that Sekhmet and other Divine Beings create their own coherence, outside of our human sense of cause and effect.)

To return to this dream summary, Bob reminds me that the requirements of my work with Sekhmet are infinitely greater than my previously limited concepts of Divinity would allow. (During the years since Karnak, I have integrated the dreams and Her Divine Being into my own metaphysical understanding.) As each of us is committed to our mystical quests, we discover significant fragments of psycho-spiritual knowledge along the path as consciousness evolves. When Sekhmet commands, "Know Me!" She is also commanding that I strive to comprehend the *principles* of the metaphysical world.

October 13, 1997: The Dreams Continue

I have been dreaming something I don't recall. I briefly awaken, but a new dream begins as I slide back into sleep. Bold black letters on a large movie screen announce: A Merchant Ivory Production (noted movie producers of the 1990s). The fanfare and blaring Dolby sound suggest a significant dream is about to unfold. The screen, however, remains blank. (More cosmic humor.)

Impatient, I ask Sekhmet, "What's the message here?"

In response, I hear kind laughter from spirit voices pealing around me in stereo sound. Then a voice in the background says, "Okay, Helena. Here's the message: There can be joy and happiness in any circumstances. And life is as elusive as the images on a movie screen."

Perhaps She is telling me that spiritual journeys need not be serious every moment. Relax and enjoy the process—as the saying goes. But She is also showing me again that everything is illusion (as cinema is an illusion based on other illusions: the illusion of life and of art.)

October 14, 1997

Before me is an immense mountain of glistening crystal, with sharp wands jutting out all over. The top of the mountain is swathed in mist, the summit invisible.

"Why can't I see the top?" I ask.

"You must climb to the top," Bob's voice tells me. "It's clear up here."

Sekhmet is standing by my bed as I awake.

"Hi," I say. "Could you show me the dream again?"

As I dive once more into the unconscious world, the entire dream repeats. The symbols now are obvious. This is the archetypal Hero/ine's Journey (which will appear several times, in various symbolic forms, in later dreams). The crystal mountain, with its glistening wands, represents the peril of the climb and the promise (the wands) of spiritual knowledge. At the same time, I recently gained new insight about this dream as I was researching dream patterns and symbols. In the Mystery Schools, the upward metaphysical path was often symbolized as the Crystal Mountain of Enlightenment that initiates were not ready to climb until near the end of their testing period.

There is an intriguing corollary to this dream: most of us are familiar with fairy tales set on a crystal mountain or glass hill that must be climbed to secure the treasure at the top. These folk and literary stories are not only thrice-told tales in the template of the Hero/ine's Journey, but are also a version of the ascending tests of spiritual difficulty as the seeker climbs to higher levels of wisdom. The narrative of the Mystery Schools' esoteric knowledge (sadly, much of it long lost) is degraded into a fairy tale in some of the retold versions.

October 18, 1997

Before sleep, I ask Her to "give me another 'real' Sekhmet dream." She does.

I am standing in front of Her statue at Karnak. The walls, no longer stone blocks, are pure gold, and golden light floods the small room. The statue is once again alive.

Sekhmet tells me to take the stethoscope out of my shirt pocket and put it to Her chest. What stethoscope? I grope through my pockets. Sure enough, the stethoscope is there. As I move closer to Her, I can feel—not cold stone, but the warmth of a living body.

When I place the instrument on the statue's chest, I hear and feel the beating of Her heart. This experience is shocking in its power, moving in its intimacy. Even in my dream, I am trembling.

The Goddess next tells me to put the stethoscope down and place my hand over Her heart. Awed by the request, I hesitate to touch Her with my bare hand. I hold my breath. How dare I touch this Goddess, Who is Supremely Divine and Whom I love so much? She lightly taps the top of my hand and shows me where to rest my palm against Her chest. Again I hear and feel the rhythmic beating of Her heart. Incredulity and devotion sweep through me. I am actually experiencing the Goddess's living heartbeat!

"I am alive," She says. "I am alive!"

Over the years, I have interpreted this dream as primarily a portrayal of the intimacy and love between a God-being and a human. As I was preparing this manuscript, however, I came across a passage from Normandi Ellis' *Imagining the World into Existence*. This scholar informs us that "For Egyptians, the heart held all memory and thought. The seat of consciousness dwelt there." The dream, thus, points us also to a major theme of the Sekhmet book: the evolution of developing consciousness.

The Introductory dream phase now comes to an end. She has put Her metaphysical principles in place, established the reality of Her living presence, and laid the foundation for the mythic Journey to come. At this point, I will temporarily suspend the dream descriptions, which will continue in Chapter Fourteen. Before leaving this chapter, however, it's timely to return to the importance of self-love and its significance to all spiritual and mystical experiences. Many splendid books dealing with these topics already exist, and I recommend them to you in the notes at the back of the book. Meanwhile, I will make seven observations about self-love.

Most of us struggle with negative thinking about ourselves, however effective our façades might be. It is true that like attracts like: positivity attracts positivity, and negativity attracts negativity. Wherever negative energy dominates in our lives, it crowds out positive people, actions, and things that would be attracted to us if there were space for them. As we already know from current brain research, we can change our attitudes through positive self-talk, images, and visualizations, as well as our actions. "Self-love is a spiritual practice," blogger Jeannette Maw says. Deepak Chopra's similar statement reinforces the concept: "The real spiritual work is to learn self-love."

Here are suggestions for transforming our attitudes toward ourselves as we deepen our spiritual practice.

1. **Read Books and Articles** about individuals who transformed their lives by learning to love themselves profoundly. Many writers have shared their private battles with self-despair and every variation of named and unnamed fear. Their experiences speak to their bleak times of the soul, as well as to the illuminated moments that opened their "receptive consciousness." (The oracle and priestesses at Delphi used this phrase for the individuals who had weathered enough challenges to achieve a consciousness wise enough to receive God-Being.)

    One of my hero/ines is Louise Hay, a founder of New Thought and of Hay House publishers. Together, she and the published works of Hay House have created a massive change in spiritual consciousness during the past twenty years. Louise herself is an example of positivity, the power of self-healing, and courage in facing adversity. Abused throughout the early decades of her life, she never diminished her belief in the power of the human mind to effect change. Not only did she validate the effectiveness of using daily affirmations, positive thoughts, and visualizations in manifesting a new world (think of how we now view AIDS compared to thirty years ago), but she demonstrated repeatedly the healing power of love. At the height of the AIDS epidemic, when even family members would not hug or touch an AIDS victim, she stood at the foot of the lectern after her speeches and warmly embraced every individual who lined up to receive the first gestures of affection some of them had been given in months or years.

    Gay friends of mine in California still describe, with tears in their eyes, the effect of her loving outreach. She wasn't the only public figure who displayed compassionate acceptance, but she was one of the few who lived the words she spoke and wrote, even after facing emotional wreckage in her own life. She not only learned how to love herself, but she taught others how to heal as she also taught practices of self-love to generations of seekers.

Two moving books about the deep nature of self-love that affected my life are oldies but goodies. Louise Hay's book, *You Can Heal Your Life,* radicalized the ways by which many of us thought about virtually everything in our lives, from cancer to ecology to compassionate love and self-love. Dr. Susan Jeffers's *Feel the Fear and Do It Anyway* taught me, and millions of others, to confront and overcome our fears of acting, being, and loving in the world. Both books provide practices to change our thoughts, techniques for replacing negative attitudes with positive ones, and daily rituals for generating self-love. In addition, the popular monthly magazine, *Oprah,* is abundant with short, to-the-point articles on love and self-care. To discover additional publications and CDs, browse in bookstores and go on the web; blogs, too, can be a wisdom source, as can other social media.

2. **Be Practical: Combine the Practice of Self-Love with the Practice of "Extreme Self-Care."** We feel good about ourselves when we feel good in general. You know the drill: get enough sleep; eat nutritious food; maintain a healthy weight; exercise; play; laugh as much as possible; attend to our spiritual lives; nurture ties with loving circles of family, friends, communities; protect your private space and time. I suggest a CD by Suzanne Scurlock-Durans, *Healing from the Core: A Journey Home to Ourselves;* it offers the added advantage of wisdom you can listen to during your daily commute. Cheryl Richardson's *The Art of Extreme Self-Care: Transform Your Life One Month at a Time* also provides sensible advice for setting up routines, lifestyle patterns, and attitudes that foster self-love and self-care.

3. **The Moment Is Now.** You and I know how it is: our thoughts fly everywhere, except the present moment. But all meaningful feelings, plans, ideas can only occur in the present. Each of us exists Now, the time where neither past nor future exist. Time past or yet to come can have no impact on this moment,

whereas dwelling in the Now keeps us in the flow of life force by concentrating our focus. As we learn to be present in the moment, we strengthen our capacity for discernment: separating that which truly matters from that which does not. As our consciousness expands, we are more accessible to the Source, as the Source is more accessible to us. Three fine books on the power of Now are Jon Kabat-Zinn's *Mindfulness for Beginners,* Eckhardt Tolle's classic, *The Power of Now* (available as a CD and a download from Amazon), and any of Thich Nhat Hahn's books (many of them now available by download). Self-love and mindfulness are, as we sometimes need to be gently reminded, kindred concepts.

4. **Keep Your Self-Talk Positive.** More than any other, our own voice carries the greatest impact on our psyches. We *hear* the words we say to ourselves with more resounding authority; we also remember what we tell ourselves (as is reinforced by recent research on the subject). Phrases such as, "I'm fat," "I'm not interesting," "I'm not good enough," have corrosive impacts when they come out of our own mouths; we believe them. Each of us not only knows the routine, but has probably said all the negative phrases. One method for amplifying the power of our own voices and thoughts is practicing daily routines of affirmations/positive self-talk, while at the same time we are also consciously replacing negative thoughts with positive ones.

This is a *practice,* remember, and it does take practice. We are training our minds to manage information with mental and spiritual disciplines enabling us to expand our use of imagery and visualizations. Since this practice has been discussed earlier, the concepts are not new. (Some readers may find *The Silva Mind Control Techniques* of interest; see the annotated notes for this chapter.) In essence, the greater our level of consciousness, the more power we can have over our thoughts. As research provides greater knowledge about the impact of positive attitudes and thoughts on all aspects of our lives and neurological systems, we know our brains respond chemically to both negative thoughts and affirmative ones. We might think of the power of self-talk or inner dialogues this way: garbage in, garbage out. Thinking about that image, we can also remember the profound words of David J. Abbott, MD: "You are responsible for the chemistry of your brain."

5. **Keep It Simple, Sweetheart.** Can't think anything affirming to say on a given morning? Start out, for example, with a few slogans from twelve-step programs. Although they may seem corny at first, they do work: *One Day at a Time, Keep It Simple, First Things First,* for instance, are easy to remember and get the flow started. One of the most compelling, yet simple, self-talk practices is suggested by Louise Hay: Gaze deeply into your eyes in a mirror (as if you are looking at the person you love most in the world), and tell yourself a version of this: *I love you so much. You are lovable, loving, and loved. You deserve to be loved. I love you, _____ (your name).* Susan Jeffers recommends writing out affirmations on sticky notes and putting them on our bathroom mirrors where we will see them several times a day. Twenty years ago, I drafted five affirmations, taped them on my mirror, and repeated them aloud whenever I caught sight of the stickies. These practices no doubt prepared my consciousness for Sekhmet's appearance a few months later.

6. **Take Action.** As I have already discussed, knowledge is not enough; we must turn it into useful action in the world. The concept is important enough to repeat in this context, and to quote Pema Chodron again, "Start where you are." You don't have to make a big deal out of it. Volunteer at the local library; walk dogs at the Humane Society; visit a nursing home; play the piano at an assisted living center; become a Literacy Volunteer; be a Big Brother or Big Sister; the possibilities are multiple. Positive action of all varieties not only feels good, it is immensely empowering. That empowerment *is* self-love in action.

7. **Forgive.** Recent research affirms that the act of forgiveness affects us psychologically, physically, mentally, and spiritually. It has the power to aid us in dealing with our own grief and anger, as well as strengthening our capacity for love of self and

the Divine. Because Love is the nature of the universe, we can live in that receptive state every moment of our lives through the act of forgiveness. Granted, the psychology involved in forgiveness is complex. Acknowledging that, I remind you that a number of excellent books exist on the nature of forgiveness. The one I recommend first is Joan Chittister's *God's Tender Mercies: Reflections on Forgiveness.*

Reflections: Chapter Twelve

Dreams and their meanings are elusive. Many of us, however, have experienced metaphorical dreams, sometimes sequentially, sometimes repeated two or more times over several nights. Biblical dreams embodying messages from the Source are usually our most familiar introduction to messenger-centered, foreshadowing or warning dreams.

1. What dreams have you had that—now that you are reading this book—may have more meaning in your life than you originally assumed? It may take fifteen or twenty minutes for you to recover some of your experiences, so allow time for the images and scenarios to emerge.
2. Have you ever prayed for dreams to provide answers to compelling questions in your life? If so, did you receive the dream information? In what form was the answer given—story, brief dream fragment, metaphor, realistic narrative, symbolic images, and so on?
3. To recall an earlier *Reflection:* Have you tried Lucid Dreaming? If so, did the technique work for you?
4. Do you now perceive patterns in your dreams that you had not observed before? If so, what do those patterns communicate to you?
5. What is your definition of self-love?

CHAPTER THIRTEEN

The Hero/ine's Journey

This narrative is about spiritual quests, yours and mine. The stories of each of our lives, if we outline them, most likely tell the tale of a journey. Our adventures during the journey disclose our spiritual identity to each of us and to the world. I love what Joseph Campbell wrote about this unveiling of our mythic lives: "The goal of life is to make your heartbeat match the beat of the universe, to match your nature with Nature."

Self-love, discussed in the previous chapter, magnifies our knowledge of that heartbeat which brings us into sync with universal rhythms (remember the dream of Sekhmet's beating heart). Our spiritual intention in the quest, however, is greater than this; it is to move beyond the self-love we have struggled so hard to embrace into the selfless space of Annihilation of the Ego. "When we quit thinking primarily about ourselves and our own self-preservation, we undergo a truly heroic transformation of consciousness," says Campbell. At this stage, we are ready to discuss the Hero/ine's Journey.

As the composer of this narrative, I have intentionally interrupted descriptions of the dream sequences until I could summarize Joseph Campbell's steps of the Journey and weave a more textured context for the dream interpretations. We can then perceive how fragments of the Mysteries and universal myths are revealed in the dream scenarios to follow. From Moses leading his people out of Egypt; to King Arthur and his Knights pursuing the Holy Grail; to the Biblical account of Rachel searching for her lost children; to Demeter descending into the Underworld to search for her daughter, Persephone; to the Quest for the father in *Star Wars,* the stories are as ancient as human imagination, yet as new as the day's sunrise.

The crux of the Hero/ine's Journey, as Campbell defines it, is the Search for the Goddess, the idealized Beloved whom we seek and whom, once found, reveals the intrinsic meaning of Love on every level, most significantly the Sacred. Profound longing characterizes the seeker on this path until the Divine Beloved and the pilgrim are united. As Jean Houston describes this longing, "We yearn for the gods and the gods yearn for us. . . ." The Quest is not a Romeo and Juliet story, but the myth of how the Beloved represents Sacred Love, which is at the heart of Enlightenment. We embrace the Quest or Journey because we must. It is our challenge, as well as a condition of honor, to be tested to our limits (knowing we risk perishing along the way), to *live* out our mission. During the Journey, like Dorothy seeking the Wizard, we discover the missing parts of ourselves (courage, heart, brain) and find the supreme meaning of our own place in the world.

Campbell and other historians of myth view the stages of the Journey as archetypal, as templates that can be overlaid on human lives to explain the significance of our own journeys. In the following summary of Campbell's points, I have merged several of the standard lists and amended the language to emphasize the Quest's universality to our contemporary world (Hero, for example, becomes Hero/ine). Campbell's outline, nevertheless, becomes real only when human, as opposed to simply mythic, experience adds flesh and blood to these characteristics. As a reader, I would want to know how these characteristics are embedded in the sagas of heroic adventures. As the "I" author, on the other hand, I was initially reluctant to place my own experiences into the characteristics. My editor, however, convinced me that my experiences were needed to illustrate the contemporary vitality of the Hero/ine's Journey, to demonstrate that the mythic Quest is a timeless retelling of the universal human need to seek, and the individual's need to find, the Sacred.

The following, then, is a list of mythic characteristics, along with outcomes of each stage of my Journey, as well, perhaps, as your own.

- The Hero/ine, an outsider to the ordinary community, receives a Call from Divine Source to undertake a spiritual quest, journey, or adventure.

As you already know, Sekhmet called me to Egypt, and then to surrender and service.

- **Initially, the Call is refused.**
  Many times, I refused Sekhmet's Call to surrender, until, finally, I realized that this Journey must be undertaken. A summons from a Sacred Being may not be ignored.

- **The Hero/ine meets a destined mentor (usually a super-natural figure, or a human with evolved understanding of the esoteric).**
  The Hierophants, Bob Masters and Jean Houston, laid the foundation for my esoteric understanding, as I have extensively described in previous chapters. In addition, Sekhmet was, and is, the supreme Hierophant.

- **The Hero/ine crosses into another dimension or plane where ordinary rules do not apply.**
  Sacred Dreaming transported me into other dimensions where Gods walk, Deities converse with their acolytes, there are no rules of time or space, where metaphors and parables are reality, where a radiant and splendid life continues after death, and where supernatural powers lead us to enlightenment. These elements apply also to the initial mystical experience with Sekhmet at Karnak, and since then. Expanded consciousness occurs when the rules of ordinary life are suspended temporarily.

- **A series of challenging tests begin; s/he cannot move forward on the path until each succeeding test is completed.**
  This aspect of the Hero/ine's Journey is also reminiscent of the seekers' transit through the Gates of the Mystery Schools eons ago. The adventurer's worthiness is tested at every turn; thus, the perilous mountains must be climbed, the vast waters traversed, parables translated, and riddles answered—all of which I encountered in my dream pilgrimage. Life or death are

at stake, this stage of the Journey warns us; to fail is most likely to perish. Simultaneously, I faced my own emotional, spiritual, financial, physical challenges in the "real" world.

- **The Hero/ine encounters an all-encompassing, most significant love.**
  Campbell portrays this as the Search for the Beloved which leads at last to encountering the adored Goddess. For me, it was being seized and claimed by Sekhmet.

- **The Hero/ine meets the Temptress or the Black Knight, a seductive figure who draws him/her temporarily away from the Quest.**
  Full Attention (see Chapter Four) is required to maintain our spiritual practices, and even the best of us is distracted by ordinary life. I surely did encounter both a Temptress and a Black Knight during a lonely period in my Quest. However, never underestimate what a powerful magnet is the Hero/ine's Journey, the call of our souls to spiritual adventures. You may step off the path temporarily, but the authentic seeker—who is also questing for her/his authentic identity—yearns for the return to the Quest and to the Beloved. Although we eventually summon the courage to free ourselves from the Temptress or the Black Knight, and although we take away many lessons necessary to complete the journey, each of us will carry our own psychic scars.

- **The Hero/ine faces her/his greatest fear with trepidation— and then triumphs through the emergence of inner valor.**
  My greatest fear has always been that I would be penniless, homeless and alone. Even the prominent feminist leader, Gloria Steinem, admitted her fear of becoming a bag lady—an archetypal image that seems especially to haunt women. For me, it came to a head at the end of my second college presidency and before Sekhmet appeared in my life. After too many years of

relentless work, and too little sleep or recreation, I burned out. When I resigned as the president of a New England college, I felt emptied physically, spiritually, emotionally and financially. Of course, I thought that I might never find another job, that I had lost all my security. The human spirit, however, is wondrously resilient. Just as the Hero/ine finds the inner valor to succeed, I discovered that I could triumph over whatever challenges lay ahead. In the midst of change, sometimes the greatest wisdom is to embrace even more change: moving across the country, starting a new business, learning new skills (such as business management and leadership coaching), provided me with a new passage to Consciousness.

- **The Hero/ine faces one final test, achieving victory one last time.**
  During my last campus presidency, I led the revitalization of a dying college. Saving that school, which had been marketed for sale, truly was a victory, and to accomplish it required every internal resource I possessed. For years to come, a cultural heritage and an economic lifeline for a small city in Massachusetts was preserved. For me, it was one final victory that affected many other individual lives, as well as mine. Since the details of that saga are given in Chapter Fifteen, no further descriptions are necessary here.

- **The Hero/ine receives a great treasure (or magic elixir), having triumphed in the Quest.**
  "Treasure" in this context refers to immaterial gifts of consciousness and transformation, more than material objects or worldly power. In this spiritual journey, a surfeit of treasures has come to me, many of which are explained in Chapter Fifteen: prominent professional positions; sustained love; opportunities to work in nine countries; meeting my Swedish family while I was consulting in Sweden; nurturing a network of family and friends; receiving numerous awards and recognition. Such treasures,

nevertheless, fade in the light of the most sublime treasures: the Sacred Dreams and the mystical encounters with Sekhmet.

- **The Hero/ine returns home and lives the rest of her/his life in honor and well-being.**
  Opportunities to continue doing Sekhmet's work are still abundant. Even now, in my mid-seventies, I am living the most amazing love story—earthly, as well as with Sekhmet. In addition, this book (Sekhmet's story, more than mine)—which was envisioned in my mind for two decades—is now published; a covenant has been fulfilled.

When we are called to, and accept, the Journey, we undertake a life of ardor and arduousness. Each of these qualities is essential to discovering our authentic spiritual identity, which is the Divinity within each of us. Our ardent spirits not only inspire our spiritual passion, but sustain our courage and bring us safely through the perils of the Quest.

Although each of us will be called to the Journey, not all of us will choose to complete it. What is the meaning of this life, if not to grow our souls through enlarging our consciousness? All seekers who do complete the Quests become Hero/ines for the Ages, supreme figures whom we remember in myths and odes, and emulate in our dreams. Each of us, then, who undertakes the Journey, becomes the Hero/ine of our own mythic lives.

Shifting Boundaries

Heroic figures, perilous quests, epic journeys, archetypes, and avatars stir our imaginations and inspire us to create unique visions that leave our personal imprints on the world. Each of us can live a narrative that, over our lifetimes, expands from the personal to the cosmic, from the known to the indescribable. This book, then, is more than a curiosity; it belongs with other mythic narratives that hold potent significance for us. I have narrated my story as it unfolded, as honestly as possible, even when I knew that your credulity as a reader might be challenged. Nevertheless, this is potentially your spiritual narrative as much as mine. Your willingness to consider these events—which, I believe, lift the edges of the Mysteries—adds to the spiritual evolution of each of us. As paradigm shifts occur, the paranormal may more frequently reveal its existence now. The esoteric appears embedded in the tissue and bone of contemporary human experiences. Many of us can believe, for example, what Eben Alexander recounts in his near-death experience; and if Neale Donald Walsch can have conversations with God, then so can other individuals. The mystic experience is not just for a few of us; it beckons to each of us.

Cultural shifts in this moment are redefining what is Possible in the future. When Deepak Chopra powerfully reintroduced the ancient concepts of the Quantum Field into contemporary thought, his teachings caught the tsunami of New Thought ideas, leaving our intellectual landscapes not only changed, but nearly unrecognizable. Let me share a relevant anecdote about Deepak Chopra. Three years ago, he spoke to an audience in a crowded auditorium with every seat taken in Naples, Florida, where I live. He began the evening by outlining basic principles of the Quantum Field, mind-body connection, and the brain's plasticity. Then he asked the audience to engage with him in ten minutes of meditation.

Here was a mixed gathering of people, not a circle of devotees— young, aging, and in between, with diverse interests and reasons for attending this event, skeptics as well as believers in greater human potential—all of whom slipped into silence when Dr. Chopra began the communal meditation. Without apparent resistance, each of us was totally present. For ten minutes the auditorium was quiet as the level of spiritual energy slowly built. All—or at least most—of us felt the power of All Possibility in those moments. When the meditation concluded, a soft collective sigh arose.

Now let's turn our attention back to Rosamund and Benjamin Zander's book on *The Art of Possibility,* and address once more the issue of *how* we think as a template for *what* we perceive as possible. That memorable night, Deepak Chopra raised many of his listeners into a Unified Field of energy out of which, it seemed, our minds could create anything. As my friends and I left the auditorium in a flush of excitement, we each held a vision of what we could create or manifest in our own lives. If we are not susceptible to failure of nerve, and if we can hold the energy of mind power—God/dess knows what we can bring into being! Einstein put that thought into words: "Everything is energy and that's all there is to it. Match the frequency of the reality you want and you cannot help but get that reality. It can be no other way." In another statement that speaks to the power of spiritual mysteries, he says, "Your imagination is your preview of life's coming attractions. . . . Choose your thoughts carefully, what you focus on will become your reality."

To start writing a significant book about the paranormal at age seventy-three, as I have done, for example, could be a daunting undertaking—or it could be the fulfillment of a long, visualized dream. That *Fire in the Soul* now exists is, for me, proof of what can be. I not only composed a book, I composed this transitional life stage as I grow older. I am now that which I always longed to be—a writer! Each morning, I wake up with a power surge of wonder.

Dr. Jill Bolte Taylor, a brilliant neuroanatomist, had a massive stroke at age forty-four. Paralyzed, left in a fetal position, and unable to speak, she was nevertheless aware of everything happening to, and around, her. Above all, she felt the energy of the people who came and went at her bedside; she could feel if their intentions were compassionate or perfunctory, loving, or detached. A few years later she wrote her gripping book, *My Stroke of Insight*, about her recovery and her conviction about how the force of energy pervasively surrounds us.

"You are responsible," she asserts, "for the energy you bring," wherever you are.

That wisdom is part and parcel of thinking about what our actions reveal to the people around us. How do we use our energy to leave an imprint of love and compassion in the world? How do we demonstrate that the power of our energy can affect the bonds of friendship, the tone of a meeting, the culture of an organization, the actions for peace in the world? By becoming intentional about the energy we embody, we can transform so many actions, events, and outcomes within our spheres of influence. Deepak Chopra, through his audience medita-tion, totally changed the energy of that auditorium. The more *aware* we are, and the more *attention* we practice, the more responsible we can be for the energy we bring to every aspect of our lives.

The Mythic Journey Before Us

The Sacred Mysteries are keys to many secrets, among them: Who are we? Why are we here? Which Quest is ours to undertake? The Hero/ine's Journey is a means of finding and fulfilling our purpose(s). Before we can do the work to which we are called, however, we must begin with who we are. To refer back to the earlier discussion about the relationship of avatars and archetypes to that which we seek, we can turn to the ideas of Caroline Myss. She links archetypes to our contemporary search for authenticity and individual identity. In *Archetypes: Who Are You?* she explains that you and I are called to "discover your true self," because, "your archetypes hold the imprint of that true self." How fascinating to realize that our ordinary lives are endowed with magnified power and worthiness by fitting into the larger-than-life patterns of myth and archetypes. In a sense, it's a mark of our cosmic DNA.

The Source allows us to perceive many archetypes within that Great Intelligence. Each of us matches a Divine vibration that is calibrated to us. Sekhmet Herself is an example of one powerful archetype with parallels to early descriptions of the Jehovah of the Old Testament. Both are figures ancient beyond time, ubiquitous and omniscient, all powerful, fierce, paradoxical, yet simultaneously representing Divine love, mercy, and protection. These similar attributes establish com-mon ground for comparing a pre-Christian Goddess archetype with the Biblical identification of Jehovah, and we perceive once again overlapping characteristics. As we can observe, archetypal patterns frequently echo one another.

Archetypes and avatars are complementary terms. For the sake of clarity, we can define avatars this way: they embody the God/dess who has claimed that individual to be that Sacred Being's unique representative. As a member of the human race, the avatar remains imperfect—but is worthy, nonetheless, to house the Divine Energies. Whether conscious of it or not, we become part of the Mysteries as we play out our avatar roles, stepping into our spiritual templates (as I became Sekhmet-in-the-World). In the same way, every book, every artistic creation, possesses its own template. Without question, this book has a template. Even when I faltered, the Goddess would not allow Her story to lapse. This is Sekhmet's statement to the world about Her Divine Self, absolutely as relevant today as She always has been: healer, keeper of Divine Order, inspirer, protector of humankind.

During this narrative, I have referred to the Hero/ine's Journey as archetypal, that is, embodying recurrent motifs that appear in myth and literature, regardless of culture or time. Our goal, however, is greater than this; it is to move beyond the self-love we have struggled so hard to embrace into a greater compassion for the external world. "When we quit thinking primarily about ourselves and our own self-preservation, we undergo a truly heroic transformation of consciousness," says Joseph Campbell. At this stage, we are ready for the Hero/ine's Journey.

Our possible quests are infinitely varied, shaped by the gods to guide us through our descent into the underworlds of our own subconscious, as well as to ascend to the Heavens. Learning from the found wisdom of other seekers, we can witness the quixotic adventures of *Alice in Wonderland* and the travels of the idealistic Don Quixote; we can share vicariously in the search to be reunited with the lost beloved (Demeter and Persephone, Orpheus and Eurydice), and cheer for the heroic human who challenges evil (Indiana Jones outwitting Nazi forces); we may internalize Luke Skywalker's search for the true father and for his authentic identity; and we may wonder at the East Indian prince, Siddhartha Gautama, who renounced his wealth to seek Enlightenment, founding Buddhism in the process. We respond, at least subconsciously, to aspects of the stories that mirror our own lives and guide us in the discovery of the missing pieces of our own psyches (the seekers in *The Wizard of Oz* find the inner treasures of courage, heart, and brain). We search in order to assemble the pieces which will make us whole. And each of us, in one way or another, searches for our Universal Home.

Sacred Dreams and the Hero/ine's Journey

We are now ready to return to the Sacred Dreaming Time. The final scenarios contain the largest number of dreams; these I categorize under an umbrella phrase, *The Hero/ine's Journey*. To a surprising degree, the dreams seem to follow Joseph Campbell's template of the mythic path, which I outlined previously. That a major pattern of my dreams is a template for this Journey suggests once again—to me at least—orchestration of the dreams by a Divine Intelligence.

Because of the overall complexity of the dreams' content, grouping them into categories—without losing major themes—has been challenging. For example, one cluster of three dreams involves "solving the riddle," a theme common to mythic journeys. Challenges for the questing Hero/ine have frequently included interruptions in the path by outside figures (crones, knights, other warriors, trolls) or great obstacles (rivers too broad to cross easily, glass mountains too slippery to climb). Answering the riddle also is often one of the challenges. Although Sekhmet is a presence in every other dream, She appears in the riddle scenarios only as a reference point; Her absence complicates my search for a solution to the conundrum. In Her place, She has sent Kwan Yin, known as a Goddess of nurturing and abundance. However, Kwan Yin acts out of character here. Appearing in three dreams over a one-week period, this Eastern Goddess demands in the dreams that I solve Her riddle, before allowing me to proceed on my path. Rather than experiencing Her as a comfort, I perceive Her as a frustrating impediment to my Quest. It is Sekhmet Whom I seek.

Prepared now to deal with the Hero/ine's Journey template as a guide, let's return to the Sacred Dreaming Time.

October 1997

When I first encounter Kwan Yin in my dream world, She is a seven-foot-tall, seated figure, leaning against a steep and stony mountain. I am prepared to climb the mountain behind Her to meet Sekhmet, Who waits for me farther up the narrow path. But Kwan Yin blocks the path, telling me I cannot proceed until the riddle is solved. After all, in mythic terms, this is simply one of the traditional Challenges of the Journey; until it is met, the Hero/ine may not proceed. The riddle is this: What are the three most important Divine Virtues or Moral Qualities? When I still hesitate after She has repeated it three times, Kwan Yin smiles kindly and helps by giving me the first Virtue: It is Virtue itself. However, until I offer the second and third virtues, my Quest is still suspended.

A day or two later, another dream within the dream supplies the dream Virtue Two. In this scenario (a dream too lengthy to summarize here), I am teaching a group of people who also aspire to learn the Moral Qualities. We are surrounded by a cluster of Goddesses, one of whom is Kwan Yin. (Sekhmet, higher up the mountain, is still waiting for me to answer the riddle.) Suddenly, emotions of neglect and abandonment fill me. Why isn't Sekhmet with me? I question. The Big "I-Ego" has taken center stage once again. However, I realize how inconsequential my Ego is in dealing with Divinity; Sekhmet's presence is not dictated by me, but by Her own Divine Purposes. In that moment, I "get" the Second Virtue: Annihilation of the Ego.

There is double meaning to naming this virtue. It is one of the characteristics of a mystical experience, as discussed earlier; and I keep smacking into the wall of this reality because it is one of the virtues/moral qualities I must learn in my personal Journey. The answer to the riddle is a subtle spiritual prod, another example of the sly wit of Universal Spirit (remember the early dream in which Bob is opening and closing the top of my head?). As I have shown you before, Divine communication often involves puns, word play, double meanings—forms of cosmic play, I think.

The final dream in the Kwan Yin sequence can be summarized by its theme, which supplies the last piece of the riddle. The Third Virtue is Acknowledgement of Our Divine Missions. The answer to Kwan Yin's riddle and the list of the three virtues are profoundly simple, as spiritual answers often are: Virtue, Annihilation of the Ego, Acknowledging Our Divine Missions. Even more important than solving the conundrum is the learning involved: each test or trial at various stages of the Quest demands not only a completed outward action, but an internalized understanding of spiritual lessons crucial to the "making" of a Hero/ine.

Although initially I did not believe in Sacred Contracts, my experiences since early childhood now affirm my sense that we are each sent to this plane for a reason. As many spiritual events and communications with the Divine have thus far been described in this narrative, another aspect of the Mysteries emerges: Each of us has a Sacred Contract with the Source and our Sacred Allies. We select, before we are born and with their guidance, the people we will meet on Earth, the challenges we will face (dependent upon the levels of spiritual evolution we seek to attain in this life), our friends, allies, and enemies. Once we are born, however, we are destined to forget the details of the contracts agreed to; one of our tests is to decipher the puzzle pieces of our sacred promise. In the process, we are given free choice to carry out elements of our contract. To repeat a clichéd, but true, statement: we are all here for a reason, and we all have promises to keep. Why should we wonder, then, at the learning experiences we encounter in other realities, such as dreams?

Certain motifs occur repeatedly in the final phase of the Dreaming Time: climbing dangerous mountains; crossing long bridges over large bodies of water; the appearance of gnomes and other little people as magical guides and allies; and repeated appearances of the Goddess to explicate spiritual lessons. These elements are right out of mythic templates. Since proceeding up a steep mountain is a scenario in many of the dreams, let's resume with one of those template dreams. Although the theme is cogent, its presentation is comic.

October 1997

During this dream, as an illustration, I am driving up a narrow, twisting road slippery with rain and mud. The windshield is completely obscured so that I no longer see or have a sense of direction. I call on Sekhmet for assistance. She tells me that I should turn on the windshield wipers! Although the windows are still smeared, at least now I can see where I am going. In my fear, I had not been using a simple tool—the wipers. Sekhmet seems to be saying, "Sometimes it is not necessary to make things more complicated than that."

October 25, 1997

The following dream is condensed for clarity and focus.

As is common in dreams, I am plodding along, unable to move faster. Suddenly, I am in the midst of a swirl of Spirit Beings, gnomish in appearance and size, who sweep me up and place me on a river bank. These Spirits (templates of all the paranormal little people who inhabit mythic tales) tell me they have found the hidden path to the bridge. They have taken on the role of allies to guide me.

"No!" I exclaim. "What path are you talking about?"

Although I try to walk away, they won't let me leave.

"Yes, you DID lose your way to the bridge and couldn't find it because a piece was missing," one of them insists. "We have found it." He hands me a large cardboard puzzle piece. "Now you have all the pieces to continue; you are ready to cross the bridge."

As the dialogue ceases, I gaze at a gigantic bridge suddenly arcing in front of me. I have a flash of clarity about our human states of spiritual oblivion: the bridge has been there all along, but I was not even conscious of it. Constrained by the literalness of my human mind, I was looking for a path, not a bridge.

The bridge stretches across miles of water, its far end lost in mist. How interesting that I have not perceived the symbolic overlap between pathway and bridge. Just as tall peaks must be climbed on our journeys, the symbolic bridge must be traversed as we move from ordinary life to spiritual existence, from the conscious to the unconscious, from humankind to the Divine. And I am headed toward a destination that, once again, is obscured; I cannot see the end point. Fog or mist conceals the reality of the present, as well as the mysteries beyond the bridge. I stand at the foot of the structure, waiting to determine when I will cross—not if, but when.

Working closely with these dream transcriptions again has been a heady experience. Before starting this book, it had been years since I had opened my journals, although the dreams were never far from my thoughts. I knew that my sacred promise to Sekhmet to write Her book had not been fulfilled. Reviewing the entries, nevertheless, brought fresh vision to the summaries and to that promise, as I discerned some connections overlooked in the past. My explanations to myself aided my journey then (and now), which was their purpose. Since many of these dreams are archetypal, however, you may respond to them on a personal level by perceiving differing answers applicable to your own life.

Any serious study of the paranormal reveals linkages of mythic themes to different levels of consciousness, since dreams are typically rich with esoteric symbols and metaphors. In rereading my dream records, I discovered two additional archetypal themes which appear and reappear: the rite of initiation into sacred knowledge, and the theme of the Awakened Heart. Both motifs are intertwined: sacred knowledge is only attained by the seeker who, having completed the stages of the Journey, already possesses the Awakened Heart. In fact, Awakening the Heart *is* embedded in the Search for the Beloved. When, in that tender dream already recounted, Sekhmet commands me to place my hand over Her beating heart, She demonstrates the union of human and Divine love that dwells in the Awakened Heart.

Throughout the Dreaming Time, Sekhmet provided lessons in metaphysics (timelessness, manifestation) and vibrant demonstrations of Her living Presence: "I am here! I am alive!" In the final dream phase, as already stated, She led me through the steps of the Hero/ine's Journey. The long series of dreams, extending for almost a year, thus presents a passage to the Mysteries of Sacred Knowledge/Sacred Love, reminiscent of the Mystery Schools' Passages. Often now, when Sekhmet commands—as She frequently does—"Do My Work," She now adds: "Tell My story." In meditations, She affirms that I am "dreaming Sekhmet back into existence," and recalling Her presence to the modern world.

The remaining dreams, which continue the mythic story of ordeals evolving into the Hero/ine's wisdom, do not require summaries, since their themes and symbols are repetitious. The vivid capstone dream, however, which occurred in late January 1998, is worthy of our attention. Although Sekhmet has continued to send an extraordinary number of dreams since then, the significant, daily Dreaming Time was concluded. But the final dream in this series—no surprise!—is a metaphor for the Journey's end. At the same time, it also marks the beginning of a new spiritual Journey.

This dream unfolds on the Egyptian desert, near the Great Pyramid, which is a central image in this scenario. The eerie magnificence of the Great Pyramid, a mythic symbol in its own right, takes on added meaning in the dream; it appears to contain the secrets of the Sacred Mysteries. Some recent scholars suggest that the Mystery School at Giza may have used the Great Pyramid as the site of the final initiation rites of life-in-death and death-in-life through resurrection. This theory would significantly shift the importance of this particular pyramid (as well as the texture of Egyptian mythology), by placing it within the rituals of the Mysteries. In addition, the final metaphorical meaning of the concluding dream of the Sacred Dreaming Time is magnified.

January 1998

The tone of this dream is otherworldly in its serenity. I am sitting on a small dune, in the midst of endless desert stretching to the deep blue horizon. The shade of blue indicates either twilight or the sky just before dawn, adding a frisson to the interpretation of the final image: Is this the conclusion, or the beginning? Perhaps, ambiguously, it is intended to be both. Sekhmet stands near my left shoulder. Wordlessly, She points to the Great Pyramid, which has just materialized a few yards in front of us. It stands alone, with none of the familiar landmarks (not even the Sphinx) around it. Against the desert landscape, the Pyramid is stark.

As the Goddess and I concentrate on the Great Pyramid, She lifts her hand to the south: "Look."

Gazing across the sand, I see a medium-sized door opening in the precise center of the Pyramid. The door is ajar; only darkness lies beyond—not the darkness of evil or dread, but that of the still mysterious Unknown. Through the trials and challenges of my earthly and dream Journeys, Sekhmet lets me know that I have earned the wisdom to continue to the next level in my Quest. The door to the greatest mysteries, as well as my deepest consciousness, is opening. This dream, I believe, holds a promise. Not only am I now awakened enough to open the door fully, but my Journey continues into the heart of the mysterious pyramid, and into my own sacred heart.

Reflections: Chapter Thirteen

Until this point (in your life and/or your reading), you may have viewed dreams as random events. As you've opened to the Possible, perhaps you now perceive your dreams to be metaphysical tools guiding you in your journey. At the very least, they can deepen your understanding of yourself and your purpose.

1. "The Possible World is deeply interwoven in the rest of the world," Jean Houston says in *The Wizard of Us*. Because ideas are always more revelatory when we can interpret them in our own words, either paraphrase this thought or write down what it suggests to you.
2. Yes, this question is repetitious of previous Reflections, but have you changed your ideas about the role of dreams in your life?
3. Do you now perceive the importance of keeping a record, or journal, of your dreams? Of your experiences in general?
4. If the Great Pyramid dream, or one similar to it, had occurred to you, how might you interpret it?
5. What does "The Awakened Heart" mean to you?

CHAPTER FOURTEEN

Now What?

"What happens now?" I asked Bob Masters after we had been working together for several months, and as the lavish dreams continued. "What else changes? What becomes of my ordinary life after these miraculous disruptions?"

"You already know," he replied quietly. "These experiences transform everything." As I recall him sitting behind his desk, me in the chair beside the desk, I can still see the reflective expression on his face as we spoke.

"So much of psycho-spiritual knowledge is incremental," he continued, "shaping itself—or being shaped—as your awareness level shifts." He toyed with the pen on his desk. "You will become more intuitive, for example—be able to sense many things before they happen. Know who is about to call before the phone rings. Have a keener sense of reading people—you won't be as easily taken in. In general, you may have a sharper awareness of everything."

"Yes, but I experience two worlds now—here, and the mystical space of dreams where anything can happen." I paused, remembering the experiences outside the dreams: angels lifting my car, Sekhmet in my kitchen, Judith handing me Bob's home phone number, and other events seemingly beyond our reality paradigms. "Or," I added, "the other mysterious events that began with the visit of the Great Wolf at my crib. Sometimes I feel off-balance, a bit unsettled."

"That's the least of your concerns, Helena. Given time, these experiences will integrate into your consciousness. You will experience an integrity of insight once you stop trying to make rational sense of it."

"At times, it's quite confusing!" I blurted out.

"Agreed. Some individuals never get beyond that stage. Many who have esoteric experiences fall away from the path—it requires such concentration and tenacity. Nevertheless, Sekhmet tells you to do Her Work—and She expects you to act."

"Why doesn't She just tell me what She wants? I'm ready."

Bob's voice was a low rumble. "Your journey is to Become, to absorb Intent in every cell, and to stretch your consciousness." Then he added matter-of-factly, "We each have to figure it out for ourselves."

This open-ended dialogue between Bob and me may be helpful to you in dealing with your spiritual experiences. Although you and I may search for definitive answers to dreams, omens, visualizations, prayers, and other spiritual practices, life remains mysterious; the riddle is not solved in this sphere.

Increasing Phenomenon

As years have passed, I have evolved a spiritual practice that is effective for me, and that provides the foundation of discipline for creating Her book and doing Her work. Just as She prepared me to tell Her story, so I strengthened my daily spiritual routine to energize the sacred task of composition. The four practices, which I will share with you shortly, are the channels for Her guidance; my hope is that they will also be helpful to you.

This narrative began after the Karnak experience with Sekhmet, when my soul ignited with brilliant images, intense emotions, and powerful dreams, which I was eager to decode. Not until months after I left Egypt did the realization of the difficulties facing me hit home. Those of you who have lived Divine experiences will immediately understand, and those of you who seek will be able to imagine the challenge. How do you describe a God/dess, the ineffable feelings S/he evokes, and the bond crafted by intimate communication with the Source? How can you interpret the paradoxical power of surrender?

The poem, "The Hound of Heaven," haunted me then and haunts me still. I understood the pursuit, even before the Sekhmet experience. As a teenager, I knew the existence of a Divine Force that could pursue me into Infinity, and even now my heart prickles with that knowledge. Yet, until Karnak, I was not ready to witness the illuminating Presence of the Beloved, or experience such focused yearning for that Great Being, even though the claim of the Beloved Presence is the alluring energy of love that animates the universe and all its dimensions. The energy is, as Jean Houston describes its cellular intensity, ". . . the atoms calling to each other in search of union. . . ."

In that union, we are Divinely claimed.

For the most part, and for most of my life, I have taken mystical happenings for granted. Your reaction may be similar to mine: if these events were happening to me (trust me, they have been occurring to each of us), they couldn't really be that important, because I wasn't that important. The discussion of self-love in a previous section of this narrative is intended as a wake-up call. During the discovery of that love, I realized that its lack is a barrier to the receptive consciousness that allows us to witness the Grace around us. In the same way, we are oblivious to many of the supernatural signs and events that are eternally present, and profuse with meaning. I have come to realize that mystical discoveries, profound as they are, can be uncomplicated at their core. Spiritual insights and transformative events do not require arcane knowledge or secret chants. Each of us is hardwired to know the nature of Spirit and our own souls, the god-cell within each of us.

Mystical occurrences appear to be increasing during this time, not only because of the rise of New Science, but because the veil obscuring the Mysteries lifts as our consciousness evolves. Certainly, more individuals are risking public acknowledgement of these phenomenon. A recent illustration is Barbara Ehrenreich's book, *Living with a Wild God: A Nonbeliever's Search for the Truth about Everything*, an account of her paranormal experiences from ages fourteen to twenty-four. This narrative falls outside her typical work (such as *Nickel and Dimed* and *Bait and Switch*, both of which deal with the flinty realities of economic and class inequalities) of this prize-winning writer, political activist, and self-declared atheist (who also earned a PhD in biology). She, too, kept written notes of her experiences at the time and, as I have done, uses those notes to describe the impact of seemingly inexorable events so compelling that she has now dedicated her life to finding answers through her search for, as she states, "cosmic knowledge." Ehrenreich, too, describes an awareness of miracles overriding ordinary events, and of experiencing more than one reality at once. Although at the conclusion of her narrative she retains a cautious skepticism, the book is charged with her curious exploration of the impact of a decade's unforgettable mystical events on her life and work.

Much of what I have written in this narrative is a validation that we are living on a hinge of history where the doorway to metaphysical discoveries can swing either open or closed. (Think of the door ajar in the center of the Great Pyramid in my final dream of the Sacred Dreaming Time.) Revelational times indeed!

Ritual or Routine

Fire in the Soul could not have been written at the beginning of my mystic adventure. She called me to live through many experiences first, highs and lows, as you know from my story. When the time finally came to write, Sekhmet was once more the Hound of Heaven. She pursued me and would not let me rest until I sat again in front of the computer. She has been at my shoulder throughout this process, and I begin each writing session with a prayer of praise and gratitude to Her, along with a request for inspiration and judicious editorial judgment. Wherever the language rings perfectly true in this narrative, that is the sure touch of Sekhmet.

Although you may be intrigued by my narrative, as well as the metaphysical experiences of others, there is no such thing as vicarious Mysticism. My purpose is to encourage you to live your own metaphysical reality, to develop your own receptive consciousness. As I have said before, each of us has a mystical capacity. God/dess Force is embedded in our DNA; we are genetically coded to seek the Divine, as we have learned from scientists' search for the God Particle (the Higgs-Boson, a particle "that holds matter together"), which scientists may have recently identified. Although not everyone chooses to be open to experiences beyond our current boundaries, we are living at a moment where the Mystical and Magical are more easily called forth. There is no guaranteed formula to evoke these experiences, but there are useful practices to prepare our receptivity.

The following routines—which have enhanced my own esoteric understanding—may guide you in expanding your receptive consciousness:

- Sacred Practice
- Sacred Space
- Sacred Objects
- Sacred Presence

These four elements are the core of a daily process for engaging your connection with Divine Being. The significance lies not just in ritual actions (such as purifying your sacred space), but in the discipline itself. Rituals, as we know from research by brain scientists, restructure our brains to reinforce that consciousness. When we commit to spiritual practices, we also make a covenant with our God-Being and ourselves: through these practices, which can restructure our brains, all aspects of our being will be transformed. I also refer you to the concluding pages of *The Wizard of Us,* where Jean Houston suggests other routines for using our changed consciousness to envision the Possible World.

Sacred Practice

From my experiences, I am convinced of the unlimited power of spiritual processes. You may already be familiar with this precept: What we believe, we practice. What we practice, we become. Establishing daily routines creates a channel of regular devotion with Spirit, through which we flow into a state of continuous Becoming.

Daily practices (such as prayer and meditation) develop habits of mind that change the activity of our brains in various ways. Although more brain research remains to be done, and brain changes during spiritual activity are more extensive than discussed here, findings so far indicate that metabolic activity during intense prayer or deep meditation reveals that the brain is at work, processing. As mindfulness practitioners, we are interested in the research demonstrating how all levels of brain wave frequency are affected by such meditation, since this suggests the possibility that we may be capable of greater control of brain responses at each stage of brain frequency. Studies also support positive brain responses related to body-mind integration through meditation. Needless to say, the processes of the brain during these practices lead to healthy habits of mind, which also affect our short- and long-term moods.

Meditation is one of the most effective practices for focusing our minds in readiness to listen and to receive information. Try a number of techniques for yourself until you find a spiritual "fit" that allows the world temporarily to drop away. When that happens, you can slip into the Gap, the space between levels of consciousness where all manifestations are possible. We read books by authors such as Richard Rohr and Caroline Myss, watch Oprah's *Super Soul Sunday*, meditate, write in our journals, and make gratitude lists galore precisely because we hope such rituals will bring us into this effortless space where nothing more is asked of us except to *be*.

Sacred Space

This is our chosen place for meeting daily with our Presence, guides, angels, messengers. Remember what it feels like to enter a beloved church, temple, or mosque: the sense of reverence—most of all, the feeling of sanctuary? When we encounter safe spaces, the neurological patterns in our brains change physically; a different part of the brain fires up, flooding us with pheromones of well-being. By setting aside a physical location that we consecrate (by whatever ritual is congruent with our Intent) for our meditation and prayers, we build an accumulation of resonant energy to enhance our Practices. An established place also invites us to ease immediately into a reflective mindset, into the Gap; regular routines then pattern our brains for reflection. Creating your personal space not only designates your privacy zone, but it declares your spiritual identity: "This is my soul's space. This is my psychic home." The size of the space is not important; the dedicated purpose of the space *is* important. In my home, I have the luxury of setting aside an entire room for my practice. However, you can work within whatever space is available, no matter how small, as long as you can creatively make it meet your needs.

Such spaces need a spiritual center—if not an altar, then a significant statue, totem, or other precious item. I use an old roll-top desk, like the one my grandfather had, for Sekhmet's altar. All of the desk cubbyholes and drawers hold incense, oils, a fire stick, and numerous holy objects gathered from my travels around the world. In the deeper drawers on each side of the desk, I have a variety of colored candles; bundles of dried sage for purifying the area; and rune stones I selected along riverbanks in New Hampshire and hand painted with rune symbols to honor my Scandinavian heritage. You can find your own unique ways to honor your heritage, if that appeals to you. Pasted on the side of the wooden altar is a rectangular sign with large, bold printing: *Sa Sekhem Sahu* (Egyptian Words of Power signifying "The Breath of Life, the Might, the Realized Human"). Bob Masters printed out the phrase and mailed it to me years ago. As I come upon it daily, I am reminded of his teachings.

Although, as already said, the amount of space set aside does not matter, the mindfulness involved in arranging it does matter. A friend who has small children and a small house has selected the end table beside her bed as her designated place. In the top drawer, she keeps incense, her journal, and several small sacred objects (a small animal totem, as well as stones from Sedona, Arizona). In the open space beneath the drawer, she has placed meditation books and her prayer shawl—sacred items to focus her concentration. The familiar act of putting on the prayer shawl for meditation or prayer marks the start of her morning or evening rituals and shifts her attention from this world to the metaphysical.

Another friend uses space on the top of his bedroom bureau for his cherished, sacred objects. Instead of a prayer shawl for rituals, he uses a cream-colored, embroidered silk stole. In another situation where space is limited, a colleague has dedicated a corner of her small walk-in closet for sacred space. A round ship's port window brings natural light into the area. She unrolls a prayer rug on the floor before she begins her meditation (or a yoga mat works fine), and she also has a folding step stool for those times when she is ready to sit for her meditation. A diminutive, three-sided table (found at a yard sale), tucked in a corner against the back wall, holds her sacred objects (which she keeps in a shoebox before and after her spiritual rituals).

Whether you select an area inside or outdoors, allow yourself free rein. The point is to have a private area that is used—as much as possible—for no other purpose, and that, when entered, immediately focuses your spiritual attention.

A simple Ritual of Consecration will increase the energetic power of your space. This may be a silent prayer of blessing, ringing bells, a litany of gratitude, your devotional mantra, words of praise to call your Divine Being, repeating your sacred name like a mantra—whatever feels right to you. Any words that come authentically from your inner self will be perfect. If you wish to add more mystery to the occasion, either choose a time in early morning as dawn is breaking or at night when the moon's allure adds to your sense of Divine Mystery.

Sacred Objects

Most of us have cherished objects we have collected over the years, items that carry the spiritual luster of precious memories. My own meditation room is filled with all my "finds" over years of travel and experience. As I walk into the space, I also walk into a lifetime of sacred memories. The revered object in the center of the altar is the statue given to me by Bob during my first visit with him. It is a twelve-inch statue of the Goddess seated on Her holy throne, holding a papyrus staff and an ankh. Before Bob handed the clay figure to me that first day, he held it tenderly in his hands, murmuring words I could not hear, but which (I later learned), called down Her Spirit to inhabit the statue.

When he passed it to me, he said only, "Paint the sun disk gold, and paint Her eyes gold and black so that She can see."

Every year, in the spring, I ritually repaint the disk and Her eyes, a rite of renewal and gratitude. Later, Bob also gave me a gold-dipped amulet of Sekhmet's head with the sun disk behind Her like a great halo, which he had also ritually blessed.

In Egypt, at Abu Simbel, I purchased a thick wooden staff, thirty-six inches tall, the entire piece carved with an encircling cobra. I use this staff to draw a sacred circle of Light around me before I pray or meditate. The cobra, of course, symbolizes the rearing cobra (representing wisdom and knowledge) always depicted on the top of Sekhmet's head. Papyrus paintings displaying Sekhmet in traditional poses hang on the walls, along with an enlarged photo of Her statue at Karnak. On the walls of Sekhmet's space also hang several other paintings, including two oils of Sekhmet created by Sandra Stanton (both are reproduced in this book in black and white), a Maine artist who experienced her own compelling dream visions of the Goddess. Years before we met, Sekhmet appeared to the artist in a dream, commanding Sandra: "Paint Me"—a command She also echoed in Her words to me, "Tell My story." These and other holy objects, I believe, help imprint Her energy and power in the Sacred Space. In similar manner, the holy pieces you choose will enhance the mystery of your site by engaging your Awareness and Attention, so that you can give your mindfulness as a daily gift to Her.

When you enter your special area, engage all of your senses; make the experience as sensually enveloping as possible. Candles (LED candles are safer in constrained spaces), fragrant oils and incense, textured prayer shawls (a long-time friend knitted the soft one I wear), rugs or wooden floors under your bare feet—all incite our senses and awaken our hearts. When each of us comes to our Divine Being in ritual action, the encounter is deepened by the vitality we have raised through such awareness.

Sacred Presence (Your Own Presence)

The most important element you can bring to your sacred space is *you*. All the spiritual trappings mean nothing without your absolute presence. The importance of *Mindfulness* appears to me again as I compose these words. Pay attention to what you say, think, and do in your sanctuary (as well as everywhere else, of course). Remember *who* you are bringing to your Divine Being when you give the gift of your Self.

Of course, you already know that Sacred Space and Sacred Objects are not requirements for raised consciousness. Those elements are delightful embellishments, like candles and incense. However, regular spiritual Practice and your engaged Presence *are* the creative and generative force you bring to Divine connection, and these are the spiritual powers that catalyze the reverberating energy of Spirit within.

Reflections: Chapter Fourteen

Since you are reading this book, chances are that you have already created a meditation or reflection area in your home or yard. Whether or not you have done so, take time now to think about how you can effectively make use of these elements:

- Sacred Practice
- Sacred Space
- Sacred Objects
- Sacred Presence

1. Where would you establish Sacred Space in your home? If you already have a designated area, describe it in your journal. Are

there changes that could make this space more energetically your own?

2. What rituals of Sacred Practice do you use in your space? Have you consecrated that space in some conscious manner? If not, you might consider saying a special prayer, mantra, repeat the Serenity Prayer, dance, sing—or whatever aids you in preparing yourself daily to enter the sacred world.

3. Do you have cherished objects, statues, stones or sea shells, and so on within your space? Are there items you might like to add?

4. Do you practice some form of Mindfulness? How might that be a useful tool for the creation of the Sacred Presence you bring to your spiritual practice? (Remember Jill Bolte Taylor's admonishment: "You are responsible for the energy you bring.")

CHAPTER FIFTEEN

Do My Work

"Do My work!" Sekhmet has commanded in dreams and manifestations.

"What work does She mean? What don't I understand?" I wondered at the beginning of our mystical connection.

As you already know, Her startling appearance at Karnak flipped my entire life within a heartbeat. As Her fire energy shot through me, I felt a psychic shift at once. When I walked out of Her room in a daze, my world had spun 180 degrees and my view of all realities was no longer certain. But I *knew* Her then, as I had always unconsciously known Her; She has always been with me. Such illumination, however, was just a drop in the bucket of consciousness. My greater transformation was yet to come.

I have occasionally struggled with the writing of this narrative. At times, my words stuttered on the page, as if there were too many extraordinary experiences and too few right words to describe them. On the one hand, the gifts of intelligence, curiosity, and discipline gave me a breadth of opportunities in the world. On the other hand, my childhood filled with domestic violence and parental alcoholism created a legacy of dread and secrecy. As our parents drank themselves into oblivion nearly every night, and as sounds of shouting and shattered glass filled the darkness, my brother and I wondered if this would be the night one of us would not survive. Had it not been for the love of my Swedish grandparents, I could not have lived through my teen years. However, as shamans and saints tell us, the more difficult the path, the more blessed the journey in the end.

Each of you has experienced your own complicated life, and you no doubt have developed your own resilient spirit. Sharing these painful events with you is a reminder that life is a mixed bag; each of us carries our own burdens. Out of our experiences of light and dark, however, we weave meaning, tapestries which depict the saga of our individual search for authentic Spirit. Light and dark, dark and light, finding the Divinity within is not an easy journey.

Since that singular event in early childhood when my Totem Wolf appeared, I had sensed there was something different about my life. I knew that I had been sent to earth with a sacred mission (even long before I knew about Grandmother Hannah's conjuring rituals). The visit of the Great Wolf symbolized that I had chosen a special Journey, one affirmed by omens, events, people, and astonishing synchronicities at every stage of my life. My life has been so crowded with adventures it seems as if I have lived three lifetimes in one. My personal journey, which could have turned so dark, reflects luminosity instead.

As I write these words early in the breaking light of an April morning, it is the dawn of my seventy-sixth birthday. My birth sign, Aries—Sekhmet is a fire goddess—is a fitting sign for me, signifying, as it does, fire, passion, and energy. Jean Houston used to tell me that my Aries personality chose Sekhmet as much as She chose me; there may be truth in that observation. I understand that I have always done Her Work: teaching, writing, leading. Although the work itself is important, it matters most when it is imbued with the spiritual intent we bring to the tasks at hand. It is no surprise that She also charged me to write this book. This has been an act of daily devotion during the past three years as I bring Her to life in this narrative. I love the word "charge" for its bold, commanding sound. Saying it aloud creates a frisson of energy. When I was daunted by the demands of this book, I sometimes repeated that word out loud, along with a favorite quotation from Julia Cameron's *The Artist's Way*: "Leap and the net appears." It always does.

Alive to the Presence

By the time Sekhmet appeared, I had already experienced a rich life: two successful university/college presidencies (later, there would be five), numerous leadership awards, honorary doctorates, international leadership involvement, and several publications. After She spun Her enchantment at Karnak, and as I turned my full consciousness to doing Her Work, that list would grow.

Sekhmet chose me precisely because I was already prepared for Her. As paradigms and our lives shift, as the divide between Divine and Human realms diminishes, as more of us share our paranormal experiences, doubtless more of us will be receptive to esoteric possibilities. The Mysterious may no longer appear strange. Divine Presence may then claim us with astounding love, as Sekhmet has done with me and others. Recalling a phrase I used earlier in this narrative, I have been Sekmetted.

One function of this book is to make Sekhmet accessible to you, as well as to demonstrate her living relevance to our contemporary world. Whether or not you respond to my story, perhaps the esoteric possibilities described may seize your attention. For myself, I recognize unshakably that the Divine Mind communicates unceasingly with us. Only our distractions prevent us from being present to the Infinity within. As a kind of learning aid (that which we "see," we can comprehend), the ineffable appears to us in reverbatory images to which we can respond. We can then recognize a familiar external form (Artemis, Thor, Jesus, Mary, Vishnu, Sekhmet) that is already familiar to our unconscious, and we vibrate to that energy. As our consciousness expands, our ability to see the Divine in many manifestations is likewise enlarged.

Although I recognize Sekhmet as my Divine Being, you may see Jesus, Thor, Isis, or some other Sacred Entity. You may find Sekhmet's lion head off-putting, but for me it is Her holy form and the sacred symbol of Her Power, Strength, Tenacity, and Courage. To again quote Bob Masters, the presence of Divine Energies "penetrate into the whole Being—body and mind and spirit, conscious and unconscious, cells and soul." She has penetrated my "whole Being," and I am a reverberation of Her energy. This is the true meaning of Her "claiming and seizing" us; She permeates every cell. To experience the esoteric in this way is to ride the wind of the wild Divine.

Embracing Authentic Self

In these events, there is no question of authentic or inauthentic Being, since God Presence simply *is* ("I Am That I Am."). We may spend our lives churning about Authentic Self and personal identity, while hiding secrets from ourselves and everyone else. Then I hit a metaphorical wall that knocked the stuffing out of me, and I had to figure out why. I was in deep shift denial because of two secrets I had protected (and sometimes just plain ignored) for many years.

When we stand before Spiritual Presence, however, we have no choice but to disclose our true natures. How often in sacred texts have we read variations of the concept of standing naked before God/dess to allow the Sacred to enter our souls. While the hidden self shrivels, the revealed self expands into authenticity. At times, given the nature of the world's judgment, we need to be wise about our private selves. However, when secrets thwart our Awakening Hearts, it is time to confront old survival mechanisms of secrets and denial. At last, I did just that.

For years, as I lectured and wrote about "Authentic Leadership: Acting from the True Self," my hypocrisy abraded my soul. I was a secret alcoholic who drank to blackout every night. Even worse, I was a female alcoholic at a time when drinking was considered a moral issue, even more shameful for women. In addition, I was ashamed and anxious that, if my addiction was found out, my very public leadership positions would be at risk (as indeed, in that time and space, they were).

You may have guessed from earlier references in this book to twelve-step concepts that I know alcoholism well. Too well. The disease is in my genes, going back through many generations on both sides of my family. I witnessed it wreck the lives of my parents, my only sibling (a Green Beret veteran who committed suicide in his forties), and others dear to me. This is generational suffering, which many families carry on from one generation to the next. Alcoholism was my inheritance by nature and nurture, and it nearly destroyed me, as it had my brother. After fifteen years of drinking, I reached a crisis.

The extent of my drinking could no longer be hidden: the dreaded morning shakes had begun.

Addiction leads usually to one of three outcomes: going crazy, dying, or getting sober. That last choice may sound easier to make than it is. Addiction has a devouring power; it's in our cells, brains, nervous systems, emotions, and souls. There are good reasons why we speak of "bottoming out" as a condition of "spiritual bankruptcy." In its grip, I was unable to love or to experience my life, but the alternative of putting down the drink forever was terrifying. By the time compassionate friends performed an intervention, I knew this was my final wake-up call. Drunk the previous night, I had nearly fallen head first through a plate glass door. Although it wasn't my first self-destructive act, I knew it had better be my last one.

For me, sobriety was magical. In the back of my mind, I knew (and I believe) a Sacred Promise was given to me in the first days of drying out—that if I could remain sober for ten days, I would be able to stay sober for the rest of my life. During those early days, I read a meditation that basically said this: if Spirit loved you enough to rescue you from drowning in the deep waves of the ocean by bringing you to the shores of safety, how could you ever believe that this same Spirit would then fling you back into the sea again? That passage, with its powerful imagery, gripped my imagination so forcefully that it is alive in my mind up to the present moment. Now I apply that metaphor to all kinds of difficult situations in my life.

As I meditated on the Promise, a revelation swept through my brain, filling me with golden warmth. "Revelation" and "golden warmth" may sound corny, but those words describe what I felt. Our lives are filled with miracles and Mysteries; this was one of mine. I knew then that I was safe, that all was well. This woman (me) who could not be abstinent for more than sixteen consecutive days, suddenly realized, with surreal peace, that she would be sober for the rest of her life.

Fortunately, I was one of the lucky ones. I made it through addiction to sobriety. From the Sunday morning I emptied the last bottle of booze down the sink thirty-five years ago, I have not touched alcohol. Through the grace of Spirit, many friends, and meetings three times a week, I changed my behavior, attitudes, and life. At a time when, nationally, women held only five percent of academic presidencies, I was one of those presidents. I led workshops for other presidents, CEOs, and their spouses about the seduction of addictions, and I helped bring the subject out of the closet (there are so many closets for hiding unpleasant truths!) and into the academic world. Even more liberating, I could speak now with my own inner authority about Authentic Leadership.

The second secret was more difficult to reveal publicly. Unmarried and female in a university presidency—thirty years ago—I continued to withhold another part of my identity—out of necessity, I convinced myself. Then I fell ardently in love with another woman. *Gay and Proud* was not the currency of the day, and I kept that secret until it nearly suffocated me. Finally I came out of that dark and musty closet—job security, professional reputation, and everything else be damned! *To know and to dare* prompted another Awakening of the Heart: when love so vibrant touches your core self, it must be acknowledged. Of course this disclosure affected the attitude of some members of the board of trustees who had hired me. Nevertheless, I confronted the storms and went on, over time, to serve as a change agent in four more campus presidencies. Because the last position is a tale deserving its own narrative space, I will share it with you later.

As I have reread this chapter, how absurd it seems now to discuss the stigma of single females, addiction, and life realities; but, at that time in the 1970s and early 1980s, those issues destroyed many women's careers. A professional frontier did exist, and it was windswept and isolated out there. A few women leaders, however, stood our ground on that metaphorical prairie, and we broke down the barriers for the female leaders who followed—and thrived!

Doing Sekhmet's work brought me into a world crowded with exhilarating events (think of being an American travelling in Russia as the Cold War was ending, when Russian President Gorbachev and his wife were taken prisoners at the Black Sea; and three days later, crossing the border between Russia and Lithuania by train to be met at the station by a young woman wearing the national costume on the first morning Lithuanians were legally free to reclaim their language, culture, and customs); people (imagine the brilliant opportunity of speaking individually, at the same reception, with Jane Goodall, Queen Noor of Jordan, and Mikhail Gorbachev); and experiences (visualize coaching the woman MD who was selected to be the first female president of Sweden's famed Karolinska Institute, one of the world's leading medical institutions).

Doing Her work opened the entire world to me, and I have lived that work with passion. As we are reminded by Rosamund Stone Zander, living our lives passionately illuminates the purposes to which each of us is born. She refers to this awakening as "Giving Way to Passion," after which nothing is ever the same. This is profoundly true, since passion permeates the Mysteries. After Karnak, possibilities flamed around me, as similar possibilities are daily ignited within each of you. An authentic life is oxygen to the Divine fire within each of us. Zander states:

We pose the question again: "Where is the electric socket for possibility, the access to the energy of transformation?" It's just there over the bar line, where the bird soars. We can join it by finding the tempo and lean our bodies to the music; dare to let go of the edges of ourselves . . . participate!

What an efficacious image—"dare to let go of the edges of ourselves . . ."! And what an exhortation: *participate!*

Compassion in Mystical Authority

As I stayed my course, I served in many satisfying professional roles. The titles and awards are not as meaningful as the presence we bring to the world through our service. Remember Jill Bolte Taylor's words: "We are responsible for the energy we bring."

These experiences converged when I was invited, along with about forty other international leaders and discussants, to spend a week with the Dalai Lama as his guest at a retreat center in Italy. Our purpose was to share our perspectives and evolving insights as teachers and educational leaders, artists, musicians, politicians, spiritual thought leaders, and change agents. While this was a forum for idea exchange, we also told our life stories, sang, laughed, broke bread together, and meditated in space safe enough to put aside our masks and public selves.

Many stories shared within the group remain vivid in my memory. Challenges such as the Reconciliation Movement in South Africa after Apartheid to heal a nation and its people, as well as tales of the geno-cide, torture, and atrocities in Tibet—to name a few—were described by participants. As the Dalai Lama listened to us, he also shared his wisdom and loving message of compassion. He was an example of depersonalized detachment, even from events in his homeland. After His Holiness lovingly spoke, many of the participants shared their sear-ing epiphanies. Sometimes, when we put words around these blazes of insight, they lose their magic. Nevertheless, epiphanies do shift our consciousness. I now understood what Sekhmet meant when She called me to do Her Work—sacred work is not simply a task to perform, but the psychic labor of compassion.

One of my private actions of compassion and reconciliation remains achingly close to the bone, as I suppose these events always are, and it is a worthy addition to this narrative. Several times I have alluded to the chaotic home in which my brother and I grew up. Since addi-tional details serve no healing purpose, I will go directly to the event that took place fifteen years after my brother's suicide. The suffering inflicted by a suicide is outrageous for those left behind; none of the essential questions can be asked or answered. There is only blank space. Because my living family numbers are small, few of us are left to tell our family histories and recite the funny, crazy, and poignant stories about the deceased, to share the anecdotes that revitalize our memories so that we do not forget who they were. Haunted by that recognition, I began a healing process with my father. When I picked up the telephone to call him after years of estrangement, wings of emotion beat wildly inside me. Maybe this wasn't such a good idea, after all. But our first tentative conversations over time flowed finally into loving acceptance, allowing both of us to detach from the past as we released corrosive, old stories.

Some events that could never be resolved could at least be put to rest. At my third presidential inauguration, Dad was in the audience. I asked him to stand as I expressed my gratitude for his gifts to my life: the importance of education, the treasure of love, and the meaning of forgiveness. Together, we had peacefully closed the circle.

Gifted Purpose

Anecdotes like these give vitality to words on the page. Since there is no better way to illustrate the mystical authority of Sekhmet's Presence than to continue telling Her stories and mine, let me share one more experience with you: the exhilarating events of my last college presidency. At age sixty-eight, I assumed, to use a metaphor from North Dakota days, that I had hung up my academic presidential spurs—although I did admit to an occasional hankering for one more call to leadership.

That call came in the form of a dying college.

Doing Sekhmet's Work

Once again turning my world upside down, Sekhmet placed me exactly where She needed me to be. As I said earlier, She typically works through surprising and unexpected events. This fifth college presidency came about only after intricate machinations—far too many to explain sensibly. However, I can give you one example of the sequences and serendipities She arranged to bring me to Montserrat College of Art, a school I had not heard of before, in a town which I was not familiar with, near Boston. At the time, I was in a transition between selling my condo in Massachusetts and settling into my house in Vermont. I made one last trip back to Massachusetts to make sure all loose ends were handled, including the disconnection of my telephone in the condo.

However it happened, the phone in the condo was still active. A voice mail message from a professional colleague was waiting for me. Giving me his phone number, he asked if I would agree to be interviewed for the interim presidency of a small art college. Time was of the essence, he emphasized. An hour later, after I had called him back and received all the pertinent information, the phone line went dead. I had come this close to missing that call and losing one of the most satisfying opportunities of my professional life. All events, including the timing of my trip back to Massachusetts and the call from a colleague whom I hadn't heard from for three years, had to be perfectly aligned for each event in the sequence to fall into place. Sekhmet's imprint was all over these improbable occurrences.

When I was offered the presidency a few weeks later, members of the board of trustees set my task: to sell the college before it went bankrupt. The first visitors to my office the first work day were the president and loan manager of the local bank holding the school's mortgage. Prospective buyers had already been approached, some of whom were interested in the acreage and the location, but not in the educational institution housed there. At my request, the trustees gave me a two-week reprieve to assess the situation and recommend the next steps.

Institutions on life support give off a palpable aura of defeat. Grief and hopelessness exuded not only from the human beings who loved this campus, but seemingly from the very bricks and buildings. Mourning had already set in. Even the leaves on the trees were dying when I arrived on campus in late summer. Despite that, I could still psychically feel Montserrat's energy, its buried life beneath the grief. This college, once thriving with creativity, did not need or deserve to die. I was touched by the same emotions I had experienced at Karnak when Sekhmet placed my hand over Her heart. Just as I had felt the heart of the Goddess then, I now felt the beating heart of this campus.

There are experiences in life where events and action must be taken to extremes in order to counteract inertia. In these circumstances, the act of leadership carries with it an electric current of Possibility. Leadership is thus imbued with a mystique; a miracle is at work in a seemingly impossible situation. This was my experience at Montserrat. Because time was short, I pulled together a leadership team and initiated a compressed set of action strategies. These began with open dialogues with students, faculty, alumni, staff, community leaders, the board of selectmen in town, prospective donors, former trustees—conversations with any individual or group who wanted to tell me the story of the school and their hopes that it could be revitalized. It soon became clear, despite the precarious financial and enrollment picture, that no constituency wanted the college to close, and they were eager to help. Not only had the school been an economic and cultural force in the community for over fifty years, but it had its own niche: inspiring and transforming the lives of talented students who would never be admitted to one of the more prestigious art schools, but who could nevertheless build their lives around the practice of their own artistic visions.

"Art Changes Everything" was the college's motto, an inspiring phrase generic enough to apply to many art schools. Yet those words somehow burned unique and bright at this college. Art had changed everything for the students and faculty, and it had immeasurably enriched the life of the community. Townspeople loved the flavor added to their village culture by students with blue or purple hair, multiple nose rings worn jauntily (sometimes defiantly), and students sitting on curbs or city benches with sketch pads in their laps, drawing with rapt attention. The environment had been—and could be again—crackling with creative energy. Following all those public conversations already cited, we had regained the attention of many constituencies, and the media. At the conclusion of two weeks, an anonymous donor gave the college its first one million dollar gift, a precursor of other funds to come.

After the trustees received my positive report and strategies for renewal, they changed their intentions about the college's future—if, that is, I could implement feasible plans for favorable publicity, enrollment growth, finances, and fundraising. By creating a culture of partnership with internal and external shareholders, all of us holding the same vision, we revitalized the environment on campus and instilled guarded optimism off campus. This was our last chance to save the school. I believed passionately that Sekhmet would draw the right assistance to the campus. She did just that.

Sometimes good fortune is inexplicable; events and people come together at exactly the right time and in the right circumstances for creation of a Force Field (as Meg Wheatley names this phenomenon) that changes the trajectory of an organization. That is precisely what occurred for the college. I recall a phrase from *A Course in Miracles*: "Miracles are simply a shift in perception." The renewal of the school was, as even *The Boston Globe* observed, "a miracle." That change in media perception served as a magnet drawing praise, hope, students, donors, and others who offered time and energy. When the college thrived, its success was owned by both town and gown. That vision was alive when I walked the streets of the town, going in and out of businesses, telling the Montserrat story—and listening to the towns-people tell the story through their eyes—as we constructed the mythic tale of the dying institution that breathed itself back to life.

Of course, the hard facts of our financial situation remained. The initial donation of more than one million dollars would have been a drop in the ocean at many campuses, but to ours it was large enough to give us options and venture capital. The end result was that this first gift encouraged other donors as fundraising events were held in many of the community's spectacular private homes and elsewhere. Because we dwelled within the energy of Possibility, by the end of the year we were able to showcase architectural plans for construction of the college's first-ever new buildings: a student residence complex of four interconnected buildings. Our students, who had participated in discussions of the interior and external design, expressed their sense of ownership and community by simply naming them "the Village." That spoke volumes about the transformed culture that had taken root during the planning process.

At the dedication of the building, I was given one of the most touching leadership gifts I have ever received: the structures were named the "Helena J. Sturnick Residence Village." After two and one-half years, a daring campus vision had been achieved, and a college was reborn.

This indeed was *living* Sekhmet's Work.

Reflections: Chapter Fifteen

The wider the arc of our reading and reflection, the more alive we can be to the presence of other realities. The more mindfully we live, the greater are our metaphysical possibilities. This fullness of perspective is what I bring to you from the years of being guided by Sekhmet. In the end, the story of a struggling art college is a story of Manifestation created out of spiritual vision, belief, and intention.

1. Questions about Mission have been included in this book's earlier *Reflections*. As this chapter makes clear, however, our purpose is not about Right Work as much as it is about our ethical presence in transformative action. What impact could these ideas have on your spiritual life?
2. Looking for patterns throughout your life, where have you felt especially guided or directed? In what ways have you received this guidance?
3. This chapter describes events which were intrinsic to Finding the Divinity within. Recall and write down which of these experiences are related to your own discoveries. What did/does each experience represent to you in your process?
4. Returning to Rosamund Stone Zander's quotation, have you found "a passion to participate in your life"? Is it significant that she uses the word "life," not "work"? Write your thoughts expanding upon what this passage means to you.
5. What does the concept of authenticity and/or authentic identity suggest to you now? Is your response different from what it was when you started reading this book?
6. Sum up—for yourself—what this book has given you.

CHAPTER SIXTEEN

Sekhmet Rising

This book is a promise fulfilled. It is a Covenant Book—Sekhmet's metaphysical display of Her contemporary Presence, not as an antique figure in the misty past, but energetically alive here and now. For millennia, She has been known as the Most Powerful One, Her astonishing miracles and synchronicities transforming our realities and our esoteric understandings. For me, among other characteristics, She can be designated the Lady of Radical Transformation, as you have seen throughout this narrative.

As paradigms shift and cultural markers transform, Sekhmet is once again Valued, Valid, and Valuable. A dynamic arc of Her energy surges through the cosmos. As Her miraculous Presence rises, She is again relevant to every breath we take. She takes Her place once more as our Divine Protector, eternally hovering over us. As we discover Her Divinity within, She calls to us with loving compassion. At times, Her Presence soothes; at times Her energy sizzles within me, as has often been the case during the writing of this book. Her dreams still continue, although they are sporadic now.

All Divine Beings are, I suspect, demanding in their Presence. Sekhmet, as this narrative suggests, is surely one of the most commanding, and Her requirements are never to be taken lightly. Walking with Her is

---

Sekhmet Rising (opposite): The third painting in the Sekhmet Trilogy by Sandra Stanton, the portrait represents a mature Goddess (the Crone) returning to life again ("rising") in the contemporary world, surrounded by the statues magnifying Her power and witnessing Her resurrection as the Wise Crone Sekhmet.

an incomparable, inexplicable experience. My best attempt at describing it is to name it "a time of incandescent exuberance and illumination."

This book is intended to evoke the *greening* of Sekhmet. Her particular Divine entelechy (the vital principle guiding development of systemic potential) is essential to our global present and future. That the English professor who prided herself on scholarly lectures, and the university president who led with such intellectual fervor, would now write these words is a spectacular psychic turnaround, ignited by this Goddess. Her Presence, consequently, has forever changed my awareness of what is spiritually "real."

Galina Krasskova, MD, the compiler of a recent publication on Sekhmet, *When the Lion Roars,* explains the Goddess's impact on her life with these words: "She is a force that cannot and will not be denied." Describing a miraculous healing process during which Sekhmet lifted her into another realm, Dr. Krasskova uses familiar language: "She claimed me." Then she observes, perhaps unnecessarily, "Sekhmet is not an easy teacher."

Indeed, She is not easy.

Moving Toward Sekhmet

This narrative is not just about my experiences. It is about the evolving consciousness of each of us. This is not my individual story; rather, it is the narrative of a mystical mind, like yours, seeking to connect with the Mystical Mind of the Ages. The story of Sekhmet is both the real and symbolic tale of the Supreme Being seeking us as much as we seek Her.

As Sekhmet enlarges Her Presence around the globe, She calls more of us to do Her Work. Due to the efforts of many spirited followers responding to that call, a Sekhmet Temple has been established not far from Las Vegas. In addition, the Church of Sekhmet continues, as well as the Goddess Temple of Orange County in Irvine, California. The latter temple temporarily housed Her massive, contemporary, bronze statue (a regally seated golden figure, nine feet tall if it were standing upright). The statue was cast in awe and honor, an offering to this once again revered Divinity, adored as She was millennia ago, by female and male devotees who view Her healing, transformative empowerment, and protection as absolutely relevant today.

Those of us who have been seized by this Goddess find each other on the Internet, in chat rooms, blogs and websites; through books and referrals within personal and professional networks; through the Goddess's presence in communal groups established to worship Her (such as the one near Her Temple in Nevada). We also connect in our home communities, and elsewhere. Simultaneously, followers of God/dess energies, some of them living communally (such as the Isis Oasis in California), are expanding the cache of contemporary experiences with Sekhmet and other Divine figures. A number of initiated Sekhmet Priestesses (as well as other female healers, priestesses, and practitioners) are breathing passion back into remembrances of these Divine Beings, who are at once ancient and new. Devotees—female and male—understand that the compassionate authority of the feminine is required to balance male energies in a universal equilibrium of yin and yang.

Some scholars are also attentive to researching the history of Sekhmet, as new archives are uncovered. Sacred songs and devotional music are composed for her, and books are published about and for Her (*Heart of the Sun* and *When the Lion Roars*, among others), reiterating the ubiquity of Her contemporary Presence.

Gifts and Challenges

Although Sekhmet's fiery energy is seductive to many seekers, I again caution you who are intrigued by Her. Her complicated and, at times, ferocious nature can send you spinning beyond the edge of gravity. Do not approach Her unless you know in your inner being that you belong to Her energy. When I stated that She claims and seizes us, those words are a mere shadow of the force of Her possession. She is a Wild God/dess, after all. Wait for Her call; at the very least, if you dare, come to Her humbly in meditation and reflection. She will tell you if you belong to Her.

Sacred Beings have always appeared to us in a variety of modalities; dreams, as we have witnessed during this narrative, are often their mode of communication. Through this channel, many of us have learned to know Her and ask for Her guidance. "Petitions to Sekhmet are not inconsequential," Dr. Normandi Ellis declares, and we must be prepared for both the gifts and challenges of Her responses.

Often, as this narrative has demonstrated, the changes She brings to our personal lives are abrupt. To illustrate: I was living in California in the late 1990s, loving the peripatetic life of an executive coach and consultant, travelling extensively to work with my clients, and certain that I would never move away from my home near San Francisco. Five months later, in one of Sekhmet's reality somersaults, I was directing a national office in Washington, DC, promoting the leadership advancement of women, and serving as vice president for a respected national educational organization. Such rapid shifts by Sekhmet are both legendary and commonplace.

The Vast Sweep of Her Presence

Sekhmet remains a complicated, paradoxical figure, Who nevertheless keeps the dangers of Chaos at bay by maintaining perfect cosmological equilibrium. As portrayed in temple and tomb hieroglyphics, She is the Great Uniter. "Most powerful One," She maintains Divine order even through the dynamics of change, manifesting Divine stability as She eternally recalibrates the universal patterns of Order-Chaos-Order.

Her many facets are expressed in the "ten thousand names" historically applied to her. Citing some of those ancient names allows us again to visualize the sweep of Her Presence. Although some of the terms are also generically applied to other Beings, Her unique Presence can not be replicated.

Sekhmet, Mistress of Life
Sekhmet, Great Lady of Magic
Lady of the Flame

Great One of Healing
Protectress of the Divine Order
Lady of the Path (Illuminator of the Journey)
Lady of Jubilation
Most Powerful One, Greater Than all the Gods
Truth Seer
Bringer of Wisdom
Light Beyond Darkness
Only One, Most Powerful One

In addition, Reverend Dr. Karen Tate anoints the Goddess with a new name (another reminder of Her contemporary relevance and inspiration) in *Goddess Calling*: "The Lady of Tenacity Manifested." As an archetypal model of tenacious courage and strength, Sekhmet "teaches us to empower ourselves . . . schools us in confidence and sends lessons our way to steel and enable us," says Tate. Perfect words to describe the process: "to steel and enable us."

I anoint Sekhmet with another designation that speaks to our Zeitgeist. She is the Innovative Spirit Who challenges us with the possibilities of continuous invention and creativity. She embodies the accelerated transformations of knowledge and consciousness taking place in our time. Eternally inviting us to new understanding, she urges each of us to *become* imaginative transformation.

With Her thousands of names, her complicated and sometimes contradictory myths, and Her lion head, She may at times appear to be an enigma too complex for human knowing . In response, let me recall an ageless Divine mantra, repeated in many texts of diverse faiths, that puts Her sacred complexity in comprehensible terms: "I Am That I Am."

I witnessed a fascinating display of Her magnetism in the late 1990s when I visited an Egyptian exhibit at the Toledo Museum of Art. Sekhmet was well represented there, with several statues of various sizes on display. Hidden behind Her larger statues, I saw the touching gifts that devotees had left for Her: small bouquets of flowers, notes rolled up into tiny scrolls or smudged, unevenly folded squares (the latter clearly from grade school children), stones, crystals, and other offerings sacred to the giver and to the Goddess. The offerings were clearly heart-gifts. It was stunning to realize how beloved She is to many individuals. One of the security guards at the museum told me the offerings were gathered up and discarded every night, but the gifts of love accrued again the following day.

After all is said and done, however, what do the dreams, visions, and gifts signify? That She is alive and She is here! She comes to us in fire and light to illuminate and protect our wounded world, reminding us that "All is well." She asserts her life force and Divine wisdom as She lifts a corner of the veil of consciousness for us. She is one of the elusive Mysteries, the answer we seek.

Sekhmet's Teachings

Although this book is not the Gospel of Sekhmet, I do want to repeat some of Her Divine teaching in order to affirm Her words within your memory long after you have closed this book. Do not forget Her!

- **All Is One.** That which is Divinely created cannot be split off from itself. That which touches anything also touches everything (reinforced by current theories of quantum physics).
- **Unconditional Love Surrounds Us.** We can trust that it will never fail us, and we can always dwell in Grace.
- **Authentic Self Is Trustworthy.** Believe in, and embrace, the Divinity within yourself.
- **Each of Us Is Born with a Unique Spiritual Voice,** a way of being in the world that belongs uniquely to us. "The privilege of a lifetime is being who you are," Joseph Campbell reminds us.
- **A Mystical Soul Dwells in Each of Us.** The metaphysical events I have narrated about my journey with the Presence can also be your experience of the Possible. Only a shift in perception separates us from full metaphysical awareness. We *can* Find the Divinity within Each of Us.
- **Surrender.** There really is no other choice.

- **All Is in Divine Order.**
- **All is well.**

I lived my life as an academic, trained as a scholar and literary critic, dwelling for many years (as I had been taught) in my head. Sekhmet, swooshing in to seize me with Her vibrant mystique, now teaches me how to be *alive*.

While finishing this last chapter, I was swimming in the pool of my Florida home early one morning. A flash of brilliant red and onyx appeared in the nearby bushes. As I attempted to see it better, the bird hopped onto the overgrown branches closest to me. I gasped at the sight of a scarlet tanager, my favorite songbird. These enchanting creatures of my childhood are now scarce, and are not indigenous to Florida. Yet there it was. For me, this was another sign from Sekhmet affirming the book and blessing this work.

Bringing this narrative to a close, with all my heart's humility, I offer these words of praise to the Gracious Lady:

> Sekhmet,
> You Whose most sacred and holy Presence
> Inspired these words and all manner of
> Manifestations,
> Who empowers us with the gift of luminous
> Dreams and
> Impassioned Visions,
> Bring us Your sacred dreams and messages.
>
> Sekhmet,
> Whose infinite Intelligence,
> Energy, Passion, and Inspiration,
> Gave rise to this sacred book
> Of Spiritual Realities,
> Lead us across the bridge into Eternity.

Sekhmet,
Whose powerful energy
Transforms the cosmic world, as well as all life,
Grant us your protection.
You, O Great Being,
Who maintains the Cosmic Order,
Holding the balance between the polarities,
Between destruction and creation, good and evil,
    light and dark,
Chaos and Order,
Remember us.

Beloved Sekhmet,
Radiant Lady of Creation,
Magnificent One,
Ubiquitous and effulgent,
Most powerful One,
Only One,
Bless us.

SA
SEKHEM
SAHU

Sekhmet, I have kept my promise to you.
    All is well.

ADDITIONAL RESOURCES

Websites of interest:

The Temple of Goddess Spirituality (Dedicated to Sekhmet):
http://www.sekhmettemple.com

Church of Spiritual Light has an Annual Sekhmet Gathering:
http://churchofspirituallight.blogspot.com/2013/08/sekhmet-goddess-gathering.html

Order of the White Moon is dedicated to the Divine Feminine Energy, including Sekhmet's:
http://www.orderwhitemoon.org

Supernaturalwiki (A supernatural canon and fandom resource):
http://www.supernaturalwiki.com

ANNOTATED BIBLIOGRAPHY
BY CHAPTER

Here you'll find all the sources referenced in each chapter presented alphabetically by author. Where a source is mentioned in more than one chapter, its information is duplicated under each chapter. Every attempt has been made to provide current URLs for websites. They were accurate at time of publication.

Chapter 1: Science of the Soul

Chopra, Deepak. *Ageless Body, Timeless Mind: Quantum Alternative to Growing Old*. Easton, PA: Harmony Press, 1994.
Our experience of Time influences our biological clock.

Doidge, Norman. *The Brain That Changes Itself*, NY: Penguin Books, 2006.
A collection of case histories illustrates how chronically injured or impaired brains have recovered because the brain is not permanently hardwired, but can be remapped.

McTaggart, Lynne. *The Field*, NY: Harper Collins, 2002.
Reveals a radical paradigm that the mind and body are connected to a vast sea or field of energy and that consciousness can be used to shape our world.

Newberg, Andrew B. *Principles of Neurotheology*, Ashgate, 2010.
Addresses the relationship between the brain and religious experience and sets out necessary principles to use in synthesizing the scientific and the religious experiences.

O'Murchu, Diarmuid. *Quantum Theology: Spiritual Implications of the New Physics*. New York: The Crossroad Publishing Company, 2004.
Introduces quantum theory as a potential source of theological insight and proposes a new spirituality that embraces the latest advances in quantum physics.

Chapter 2: Beginnings

"Allies and the Occult: Best Kept Secrets of World War Two" at *Yesterday's Lies* <http://tickergrail.blogspot.com/2012/01/allies-and-occult.html> Accessed May 29, 2015.
Describes the battle between good and evil during World War II and the secretive and frequent use of psychics and divination practices by the Allies in an underground supernatural war against the enemies of freedom and democracy.

British Broadcasting Corporation (BBC), *The Nazis: A Warning from History,* (Documentary mini-series, 6 parts), 1997.
Examination of how a cultured people fell under Hitler's spell and allowed his rise to power.

Colmer, Michael. *Churchill's Witch,* eBook as a PDF.
Describes the life and work of Helen Duncan, Scottish housewife, who used her psychic abilities to aid World War II war efforts.

"Death of Adolf Hitler" at Wikipedia <http://en.wikipedia.org/wiki/Death_of_Adolf_Hitler> Accessed May 29, 2015.
Records the preceding events, up to the suicides of Eva Braun and Adolf Hitler at the Fuhrerbunker in Berlin, and the aftermath including speculation that the remains were not that of the Nazi leader.

"Eastern Star Rituals Degrees and Secrets Exposed" at *Evangelical Truth* <www.evangelicaltruth.com/ES.htm> Accessed May 29, 2015.
Describes the origins and membership requirements of one of the largest fraternal organizations in the world, including the cryptic teachings and connections to Cabalism.

Gilbert, Derek. "VFTB 097: The Allies and the Occult" at *View from the Bunker* blog January 8, 2012 <http://vftb.net/?p=4430> Accessed May 31, 2015.
Describes how Allies used the paranormal to counter Axis reliance on occult teaching in shifting the stakes during World War II.

Hall, Allen. "'Spiritual castle home' of infamous SS opens to public with £8m exhibition" at *Daily Mail* online, 23 March 2010. <http://www.dailymail .co.uk/news/article-1259803/SS-castle-Nazi-murderer-Himmler-round-table-knights-open-public.html> Accessed May 29, 2015.
Reports on opening of Wewelsburg Castle as a museum. Recounts history of the Nazi SS using it as staging area to plan the occupation of Eastern Europe at the "round table" in the "knights' room," where pagan rituals were held and Nazi plans were developed to establish the castle as an officer training school and a "spiritual center" for the Nazi regime.

History Channel. *Third Reich: The Rise & Fall* (documentary), 2010.
Uses rarely seen film footage and never-before-seen home movies and Nazi propaganda films to provide an inside view of Germany during the 1920s, '30s, and early '40s to create a nuanced and authentic portrait of the Third Reich and its people.

Hochschild, Adam. *The War to End All Wars: A Story of Loyalty and Rebellion, 1914–1918*. New York: Mariner Books (reprint edition), New York, 2012.
Eye-opening account of unsung hero/ines of World War I, who opposed the war, refused to fight in it, or tried to end it, including influential women, Irish freedom fighters, wealthy businessmen, and patriotic journalists, writers, and monarchs.

Lemons, Stephen. "Hitler's Clairvoyant" at *Salon.com*, February 27, 2002. <http://www.salon.com/2002/02/27/hanussen/> Accessed May 31, 2015.
Relates Hitler's interest in the occult and the facts and events of his use of Jewish clairvoyant Erik Jan Hanussen, who predicted the Fuhrer would become Reich Chancellor.

"Nazis Take Czechoslovakia" at the *History Place*. <http://www.historyplace .com/worldwar2/triumph/tr-czech.htm> Accessed May 29, 2015.
Details events (and photos) of "liquidation of the remainder of Czechoslovakia" three weeks after Hitler signed the Munich Agreement (stating the Sudetenland would be the "last territorial demand" of Germany in Europe).

Pike, Albert. *The Book of the Words*, Kessinger Publishing, 2005. Available as eBook in free PDF at http://www.pdfdrive.netthe-book-of-the-words-hermetics-resource-site-e214144.html
Facsimile reproduction of originally published guidebook to the words and symbols (including correct spelling) for the Scottish Rite's Masonic Order for first through thirtieth degrees.

"Thule Society (aka Brotherhood of Death Society)" at *Forbidden Knowledge*. <http://www.theforbiddenknowledge.com/hardtruth/thulesociety.htm> Accessed May 29, 2015.
Brief article about one of the secret societies that influenced Adolf Hitler and helped establish the "New World Order" of his regime.

"Walpurgisnacht, Odin, and Hitler" at *Celebrating Time* blog, April 30, 2009. <https://celebratingtime.wordpress.com/2009/04/30/walpurgisnacht-odin-and-hitler/> Accessed May 31, 2015.
Recounts the significance in German folklore of Hitler's death on April 30.

"World War Two and Eastern Europe." *HistoryLearningSite.co.uk. 2014.* <http://www.historylearningsite.co.uk/eastern_europe_world_war_two.htm> Accessed May 31, 2015.
Includes articles and coverage of various battles and sieges for occupation in Eastern Europe.

Yenne, Bill. *Hitler's Master of the Dark Arts: Himmler's Black Knights and the Occult of the SS*. Zenith Press, Minneapolis, 2011. (Kindle eBook)
An account of the Nazi Party's bizarre interpretation of ancient pagan rituals blended with Spiritualism, Mysticism, and Saxon traditions to create an ideology of Aryan superiority and the direction Heinrich Himmler took the Schutzstaffel (SS) as Black Knights, attempting to create a Nazi Camelot.

Zander, Rosamund Stone and Benjamin Zander. *The Art of Possibility: Transforming Professional and Personal Life*. Boston: Harvard Business School Press, 2000.
Provides breakthrough practices for tapping into creativity by shifting thinking toward productive new definitions about what is possible in life.

Chapter 3: Statue with the Breath of Life

Alexander, Eben. *Proof of Heaven: A Neurosurgeon's Journey into the Afterlife*, NY: Simon & Schuster, 2012.
First-person account of near-death experience of a man of science, and his miraculous recovery and transformation due to the experience.

Fitzgerald, Roisin. *Taking Heaven Lightly: A Near Death Experience Survivor's Story and Inspirational Guide to Living in the Light*. Ireland: Hatchette Books, 2015.
Told in the first person, Fitzgerald describes her out-of-body experience during a brain hemorrhage; she is filled with the proverbial light and radiance. She transforms her life from a career at the European Bank to success as an internationally known artist so that she can share her experiences of love and light.

Greyson, Bruce, MD, and Debbie James, MSN, and Janice Miner-Holden, EdD, co-editors. *The Handbook of Near-Death Experiences: Thirty Years of Investigation*. New York: Praeger, 2009.
Experts from around the world explore the controversies and history of near-death experience (NDE) knowledge.

Hall, Manly P. *Secret Teachings of All Ages*. New York: Tarcher, 1975.
Originally published in 1928 as a vast encyclopedia of the occult in an effort to keep alive ancient modes of knowledge.

Masters, Robert. *The Goddess Sekhmet: Psycho-Spiritual Exercises of the Fifth Way*. Ashland, OR: White Cloud Press, 2002.
Profound study of the wisdom of Ancient Egypt and, in particular, the powerful Goddess Sekhmet, provided through the lens of contemporary studies in psychology and religion. Includes details about the Egyptian theory of the Five Bodies as well as Sekhmet's myths, Sacred Names, and rites.

Mesle, Robert C. *Process-Relational Philosophy*. West Conshohocken: Templeton Press, 2008.
An introduction to process thought, breaks down the theories and complex writings of Alfred North Whitehead; provides a foundation for

contemporary philosophy and theology. Integrates science, including evolutionary biology, physics, philosophy of mind, and environmental ethics, with religion and theology, as well as education, politics, and economics.

Stace, W. T. *The Teachings of the Mystics*. NY: New American Library, 1960. Comprehensive overview of Mysticism and mystical experiences. Lays out a psychology, as well as a philosophy, about Mysticism and provides characteristics of mystical events, including a variety of written accounts of such experiences across religious traditions.

Stahlman, Sandra. "William James" at *Defining Mysticism* website http://sandra .stahlman.com/james.html. "A Brief Commentary" by Stahlman is included under the section "On the Varieties of Religious Experience: A Study of Human Nature" on the website.
Discusses key principles established by William James and based on the following books: James, William. *Varieties of Religious Experience* (originally published 1901), and *Understanding Mysticism* (reprinted), Garden City, NY: Image Books, 1980.

Walsch, Neale Donald. *Conversations with God: An Uncommon Dialogue*. NY: Putnam, 1995.
Matter-of-fact wisdom about how to get by in life by remaining "real" or true to yourself and your spirituality. The narrative of a frustrated regular guy who wrote out his questions to God and realized they were being answered.

William James, "A Suggestion about Mysticism," *The Journal of Philosophy, Psychology and Scientific Methods*, Vol. 7, No. 4. (Feb. 17, 1910), pp. 85-92. Discusses intuition as an extension of the "field of consciousness" and explores revelations of reality during mystical experiences.

Williamson, Marianne. *A Return to Love: Reflections on the Principles of A Course in Miracles*. NY: Harper, 1996.
Demonstrates how love is a driving force and key to inner peace in our lives.

Chapter 4: Show Me How to Do This

Carlyle, Thomas. "The Philosophy of Clothes" from *Sartor Resartus* in Outline of Great Books at The Public Bookshelf site. <http://www.publicbookshelf.com/public_html/Outline_of_Great_Books_Volume_I/thomascar_caj.html> Accessed May 31, 2015.
Through story form, the problem behind where truth is to be found is explored through the imaginary "Philosophy of Clothes," targeting the phenomena that history and cultures continually reconstruct themselves through changing fashion, power structures, and faith systems.

Chodron, Pema. *Start Where You Are: A Guide to Compassionate Living.* Boston: Shambhala, 1994.
Down-to-earth guidance on how to embrace the painful moments of our lives as a starting point for cultivating fearlessness and awakening a compassionate heart.

Eliot, T. S. Collection of works. <http//www.bartleby.com/people/Eliot-Th.html> Four volumes of collected essays and poems by T. S. Eliot available for reading online.

Strayed, Cheryl. *Wild: From Lost to Found on the Pacific Crest Trail.* NY: Knopf, 2012.
A challenging physical journey becomes a mythic life journey of spiritual and mental transformation.

Williamson, Marianne. *A Return to Love: Reflections on the Principles of a Course in Miracles.* NY: Harper, 1996.
Demonstrates how love is a driving force and key to inner peace in our lives.

Chapter 5: Mystery of Mysteries

Alexander, Eben. *Proof of Heaven: A Neurosurgeon's Journey into the Afterlife.* NY: Simon & Schuster, 2012.
First-person account of near-death experience of a man of science and his miraculous recovery and transformation due to the experience.

Bailey, Ned. "The Holy Spirit in Us" at *Starting with God* website <http://www
.startingwithgod.com/knowing-god/holy-spirit/> Accessed May 31, 2015.
Scriptures used to confirm that Spirit dwells within each of us and learning how to pay attention to It.

Connelly, Joan Breton. *Portrait of a Priestess: Women and Ritual in Ancient
Greece.* Princeton, NJ: Princeton University Press, 2009.
A historical presentation of priestess-goddesses, particularly the indwell-
ing spirits of Athena, Polias-Athena, Demeter, Kore, Eleusis at Delphi.

Franklin, R. W., Ed. *The Poems of Emily Dickinson: Reading Edition.* "Tell All
the Truth," #1263. Cambridge: The Belknap Press of Harvard University
Press, 1999.

Hall, Manley P. *Secret Teachings of All Ages.* New York: Tarcher, 1975.
Originally published in 1928 as a vast encyclopedia of the occult in an
effort to keep alive ancient modes of knowledge.

Houston, Jean. *Mystical Dogs.* New York: New World Library, 2012.
Identifies how dogs, with their uncomplicated and joyous natures, are
not only guardians of our souls but often the best spiritual teachers.

Masters, Robert. *The Goddess Sekhmet: Psycho-Spiritual Exercises of the
Fifth Way.* Ashland, OR: White Cloud Press, 2002.
Profound study of the wisdom of Ancient Egypt and, in particular, the
powerful Goddess Sekhmet, provided through the lens of contemporary
studies in psychology and religion. Includes details about the Egyptian
theory of the Five Bodies, as well as Sekhmet's myths, Sacred Names,
and rites.

Mesle, Robert C. *Process-Relational Philosophy.* West Conshohocken:
Templeton Press, 2008.
An introduction to process thought; breaks down the theories and
complex writings of Alfred North Whitehead; provides a foundation for
contemporary philosophy and theology; integrates science, including evolutionary biology, physics, philosophy of mind, and environmental ethics
with religion and theology, as well as education, politics, and economics.

Torrey, R. A. *The Person and Work of The Holy Spirit*, CreateSpace, 2011. Chronicles a collection of fiction and nonfiction classics by the greatest writers of the world and includes pivotal, but overlooked, pieces to create a broad spectrum of understanding.

Wade, Nicholas. "Evolution of the God Gene," *The New York Times,* November 14, 2009, page WK3. *The New York Times* Week in Review at http://www .nytimes.com/2009/11/15/weekinreview/12wade.html?_r=0 Accessed May 30, 2014.
Article about archaeological discoveries providing evidence that religion exists as part of natural selection and is universal because it is wired into our neural circuitry.

Chapter 6: What Is True?

Masters, Robert. *The Goddess Sekhmet: Psycho-Spiritual Exercises of the Fifth Way.* Ashland, OR: White Cloud Press, 2002.
Profound study of the wisdom of Ancient Egypt and, in particular, the powerful Goddess Sekhmet, provided through the lens of contemporary studies in psychology and religion and including details about the Egyptian theory of the Five Bodies, as well as Sekhmet's myths, Sacred Names, and rites.

Myss, Caroline. *Spiritual Madness: The Necessity of Meeting God in Darkness,* (audio book) at www.amazon.co.uk/Spiritual-Madness-Necessity-Meeting-Darkness/dp/
By the author of *Sacred Contracts*, this audio session describes a contemporary path open to anyone seeking mystical experiences and how to end spiritual confusion.

Chapter 7: My Spiritual Neter

Clinton, Hillary Rodham. *It Takes a Village.* NY: Simon & Schuster, 2006.
Expresses care and concern for the children of today's world and offers ideas for developing our society into one that works together as a kind of village that values children's unique contributions.

Masters, Robert. *The Goddess Sekhmet: Psycho-Spiritual Exercises of the Fifth Way.* Ashland, OR: White Cloud Press, 2002.
Profound study of the wisdom of Ancient Egypt and, in particular, the powerful Goddess Sekhmet, provided through the lens of contemporary studies in psychology and religion and including details about the Egyptian theory of the Five Bodies, as well as Sekhmet's myths, Sacred Names, and rites.

"Prehistoric Art in France," at *France This Way* website <http://www.francethis way.com/culture/prehistoric-art-france.php> Accessed May 31, 2015.
Recounts the astonishing achievement (and locations) of cave paintings and their impact on the start of French art.

Chapter 8: How Sekhmet Rolls

Alexander, Eben. *Proof of Heaven: A Neurosuregon's Journey into the Afterlife.* NY: *Simon &* Schuster, 2012.
First-person account of near-death experience of a man of science and his miraculous recovery and transformation due to the experience.

The Book of the Dead. The Hieroglyphic Transcript and English Translation for the Papyrus of Ani, Introduction by E.A. Wallis Budge. New York: Gramercy Books, 1995 edition. An Egyptian funerary scroll on papyrus that includes prayers, spells, and incantations intended to assist with the deceased's journey through the underworld into the afterlife. Reproductions and translations are most often of the 3,500-year-old Papyrus of Ani, one of the most beautiful scrolls discovered.

Cameron, Julia. *The Artist's Way.* New York: Tarcher, 2002.
Building on the concept that creative expression is the natural direction of life, and that creativity is linked with spirituality, this twelve-week program assists in the recovery and development of artistic confidence and productivity.

Ellis, Normandi. <http://www.normandiellis.com>
Author of numerous books on the mysteries, history, and goddesses of Ancient Egypt.

Kant, Candace C., and Anne Key, eds. *Heart of the Sun: An Anthology in Exaltation of Sekhmet* (Kindle edition eBook), iUniverse, 2011.
A collection of vast and varied encounters people have had with the Goddess Sekhmet, including prayers, meditations, and poems.

Masters, Robert. *The Goddess Sekhmet: Psycho-Spiritual Exercises of the Fifth Way.* Ashland, OR: White Cloud Press, 2002.
Profound study of the wisdom of Ancient Egypt and, in particular, the powerful Goddess Sekhmet, provided through the lens of contemporary studies in psychology and religion. Includes details about the Egyptian theory of the Five Bodies, as well as Sekhmet's myths, Sacred Names, and rites.

Wade, Nicholas. "Evolution of the God Gene," *The New York Times,* November 14, 2009, page WKE. <http://www.nytimes.com/2009/11/15/weekinreview/12wade.html?_r=O> Accessed May 30, 2014.
Article about archaeological discoveries providing evidence that religion exists as part of natural selection and is universal because it is wired into our neural circuitry.

Chapter 9: Leaping into the Deep

"10 Things You Can Do Today to Attract Positive Energy," at *Out of Stress: Your Guide to a Stress-Free and Healthy Life Naturally.* <http://www.outofstress.com/attract-positive-energy/> Accessed May 31, 2015.
Focuses on choice to be either at peace or resistant and ten actions/steps to choose the former.

Beattie, Melody. *Playing It by Heart: Taking Care of Yourself No Matter What.* Center City: Hazelden, 1999.
Personal essays, inspiring anecdotes, and prescriptive reminders help readers understand what drives them back into the grasp of co-dependent or controlling behavior and how to return to faith and healing.

Chodron, Pema. *Start Where You Are: A Guide to Compassionate Living.* Boston: Shambhala, 1994.
Down-to-earth guidance on how to embrace the painful moments of our lives as a starting point for cultivating fearlessness and awakening a compassionate heart.

Chittister, Joan. *God's Tender Mercies: Reflections on Forgiveness.* New London, CT: Twenty-Third Publications, 2010.
A spiritual treatise on the virtue of mercy and its connection to forgiveness.

Ellis, Normandi. *Imagining the World into Existence: An Ancient Egyptian Manual of Consciousness.* Rochester, VT: Bear & Company, 2012.
An examination of how the power of language, including the layered meanings of hierglyphic thinking, create reality and deepen consciousness.

Glanville, John. www.dreaminterpretation-dictionary.com/history-of-dream-interpretation.

Hay, Louise. *You Can Heal Your Life.* Carlsbad, CA: Hay House Publishing, 1994.
Decades-long bestseller on using the mind to overcome self-hatred and doing the "mental work" to heal. Describes the mind-body connection and includes a directory of ailments, related thoughts, and affirmations to alter thoughts toward healing.

Healers Journal, The. <http://www.thehealersjournal.com> Accessed May 31, 2015.
Online journal dedicated to empowering readers to understand the relationship between mind, body, and spirit and helping them transform their lives.

"How Negative Energy Affects Your Life and How to Clear It" at *Social Consciousness* blog. <http://www.social-consciousness.com/2013/09/how-negative-energy-affects-your-life-and-how-to-clear-it.html> Accessed May 31, 2015.
How to identify the level of negative energy or negative thinking we harbor, and a three-step process to clear negativity and create a positive outlook.

Kabat-Zinn, Jon and Thich Nhat Hanh. *Full Catastrophe Living: Using the Wisdom of Your Body and Mind to Face Stress, Pain and Illness*. New York: Delta Trade Paperback, 1991.
How to use mindfulness-based stress reduction techniques to soothe and heal your body, mind, and spirit.

Maw, Jeanette. "Self-love is Key" at <selfloveiskey.com> Accessed May 29, 2015.
Self-love as the missing ingredient for manifesting life's desires.

Richardson, Cheryl. *The Art of Extreme Self-Care: Transform Your Life One Month at a Time*. NY: Hay House, 2009.
Divided into twelve chapters, each chapter presenting a strategy for transforming your life incrementally in developing practical, action-focused, self-care programs that fit your own life.

Tolle, Eckhart. *The Power of Now: A Guide to Spiritual Enlightenment*. Vancouver, BC: Namaste Publishing, 2004.
Packs information and inspirational ideas into a clear and supportive message about the importance of living in the moment, the power behind the mind (our thoughts), and guides readers on a spiritual journey of true self-discovery.

Wiggin, Amary. "How to Be Nicer . . . to Yourself," February 12, 2013, at *Women's Health Magazine* online <http://www.womenshealthmag.com/life/how-to-be-nicer-to-yourself> Accessed May 31, 2015.
Why self-compassion and self-kindness is vital to mental health, and tips for treating yourself as gently as you would a kitten.

Chapter 10: Initiation into Sacred Dreams

Cameron, Julia. *The Artist's Way*. New York: Tarcher, 2002.
Building on the concept that creative expression is the natural direction of life, and that creativity is linked with spirituality, this twelve-week program assists in the recovery and development of artistic confidence and productivity.

Ellis, Normandi. <http://www.normandiellis.com/>
Author of numerous books on the mysteries and goddesses of Ancient Egypt.

Ellis, Normandi. *Imagining the World into Existence: An Ancient Egyptian Manual of Consciousness.* Rochester, VT: Bear & Company, 2012. An examination of how the power of language, including the layered meaning of hierglyphic thinking, can create reality and deepen consciousness.

James, William. "A Suggestion about Mysticism," *The Journal of Philosophy, Psychology and Scientific Methods,* Vol. 7, No. 4. (Feb. 17, 1910), pp. 85-92. Discusses intuition as an extension of the "field of consciousness" and explores revelations of reality during mystical experiences.

Kant, Candance C. and Anne Key, eds. *Heart of the Sun: An Anthology in Exaltation of Sekhmet.* Bloomington, IN: iUniverse, Inc., 2011.
A collection of personal perspectives by modern devotees of the Goddess Sekhmet.

Masters, Robert. *The Goddess Sekhmet: Psycho-Spiritual Exercises of the Fifth Way.* Ashland, OR: White Cloud Press, 2002.
Profound study of the wisdom of Ancient Egypt and, in particular, the powerful Goddess Sekhmet, provided through the lens of contemporary studies in psychology and religion. Includes details about the Egyptian theory of the Five Bodies, as well as Sekhmet's myths, Sacred Names, and rites.

Silva, Jose. *Silva Mind Control Techniques.* New York: Pocket Books, 1977. Techniques and programs for using your mind, through guided imagery and mental training, to achieve life goals.

Talbot, Michael. *The Holographic Universe: The Revolutionary Theory of Reality.* New York: Harper Perennial, 2011.
Classic treatise on the frontiers of physics and explaining the paranormal abilities of the mind, the unsolved riddles of brain and body, and the true nature of the universe.

Chapter 11: Dreams as Divine Communication

Reynolds, Lisa. "Lucid Dreaming Techniques" at *Dream is Destiny: Best Lucid Dreaming Techniques* site <http://best-lucid-dreaming-techniques.com> Accessed May 31, 2015. Describes techniques to become aware and gain control of dreams, including dream journals, word triggers, and wake-to-bed techniques.

Turner, Rebecca. "Lucid Dreaming Techniques for Beginners" at *World of Lucid Dreaming* website <http://www.world-of-lucid-dreaming.com/lucid-dreaming-techniques.html> Accessed May 31, 2015.
Top lucid dreaming techniques ranging from simple memory exercises to specialized meditation.

Chapter 12: Consciousness Awakens

Hay, Louise. *You Can Heal Your Life*. Carlsbad, CA: Hay House Publishing, 1994.
Decades-long bestseller on using the mind to overcome self-hatred and doing the "mental work" to heal. Describes the mind-body connection and includes a directory of ailments, related thoughts, and affirmations to alter thoughts toward healing.

Jeffers, Susan. *Feel the Fear . . . And Do It Anyway*. New York: Ballantine Books, 1986 (20th anniversary edition, 2006).
Offers a clear-cut plan for action to conquer fear and replace it with attitudes of strength and conviction using positive thinking and situational exercises to examine our fear responses.

Kabat-Zinn, Jon and Thich Nhat Hanh. *Full Catastrophe Living: Using the Wisdom of Your Body and Mind to Face Stress, Pain and Illness*. New York: Delta Trade Paperback, 1991.
How to use mindfulness-based stress reduction techniques to soothe and heal your body, mind, and spirit.

Maw, Jeanette. Self-love is Key at <selfloveiskey.com> Accessed May 29, 2015.
Self-love as the missing ingredient for manifesting life's desires.

Richardson, Cheryl. *The Art of Extreme Self-Care: Transform Your Life One Month at a Time*. NY: Hay House, 2009.
Divided into twelve chapters, each chapter presenting a strategy for transforming your life incrementally in developing practical, action-focused, self-care programs that fit your own life.

Scurlock-Durana, Suzanne. *Healing From the Core: A Journey Home to Ourselves*, Healing from the Core: Reston, VA, Audio CD series, 2000.
Teaches how to create from love rather than fear, including techniques for understanding your unique energy flow, setting healthy boundaries, rejuvenating ourselves, returning to center, and discovering more joy in daily life.

Silva, Jose. *Silva Mind Control Techniques*. New York: Pocket Books, 1977.
Techniques and programs for using your mind, through guided imagery and mental training, to achieve more effective and deeper mental functioning, awake or asleep. This method also suggests that help can be attained from guides on the Other Side.

Talbot, Michael. *The Holographic Universe: The Revolutionary Theory of Reality*. New York: Harper Perennial, 2011.
Classic treatise on the frontiers of physics and explaining the paranormal abilities of the mind, the unsolved riddles of brain and body, and the true nature of the universe.

Tolle, Eckhart. *The Power of Now: A Guide to Spiritual Enlightenment*. Vancouver, BC: Namaste Publishing, 2004.
Packs information and inspirational ideas into a clear and supportive message about the importance of living in the moment, the power behind the mind (our thoughts), and guides readers on a spiritual journey of true self-discovery.

Chapter 13: The Hero/ine's Journey

Campbell, Joseph. *The Hero with a Thousand Faces*. New York: New World Library, 2008.
Originally published in 1949, this analysis of the significance of myth combines insights of modern revolutionary understanding of comparative

mythology and outlines the Hero/ine's Journey, a universal motif of adventure and transformation that runs through virtually all of the world's mythic traditions.

Chopra, Deepak. *Quantum Healing: Exploring the Frontiers of Mind/Body Medicine*. New York: Bantam, 1989.
Uses accounts of seemingly miraculous recoveries from cancer and other serious illnesses to describe an extraordinary new approach to healing.

Chopra, Deepak. *Unconditional Life: Discovering the Power to Fulfill Your Dreams*. New York: Bantam, 1991.
Brings together disciplines ranging from modern physics and neuroscience to the ancient traditions of Indian wisdom to show how our perceptions create our reality for good or ill—and how the outside world can be shaped by altering the world within.

Conrad, Joseph. *Heart of Darkness*. Claremont, CA: Coyote Canyon Press, 2007.
Originally published in *Blackwood's Edinburgh Magazine* in 1899 and published in book form in 1902, this novella is considered one of the world's great books, addressing the ambiguity of good and evil. Loosely based on Conrad's journey to rescue a company agent from a remote station in the heart of the Congo, the experience calls into question all of his assumptions about civilization and human nature.

Houston, Jean. *The Wizard of Us: Transformational Lessons from Oz*. New York: Atria Books/Beyond Words, 2012.
Uses the familiar characters of Dorothy and the Wizard in the well-known story of Oz to describe the archetypes of heart, mind, and courage hidden within each of us and provides exercises to help each of us connect with our own Hero's Journey.

Myss, Caroline. *Archetypes: Who Are You?* New York: Hay House, 2013.
Delves into the universal patterns of behavior that, once discovered, help us better understand ourselves and our place in the world.

Strayed, Cheryl. *Wild: From Lost to Found on the Pacific Crest Trail*. New York: Knopf, 2012.
A challenging physical journey becomes a mythic life journey of spiritual and mental transformation.

Taylor, Jill Bolte. *My Stroke of Insight*. New York: Plume, 2006.
Chronicles how a brain scientist's own stroke became a blessing and a revelation, leading her to enlightenment by teaching her that by "stepping to the right" of our left brains, we can uncover feelings of well-being that are often sidelined by negative "brain chatter" of the left side.

Zander, Rosamund Stone and Benjamin Zander. *The Art of Possibility: Transforming Professional and Personal Life*. Boston: Harvard Business School Press, 2000.
Provides breakthrough practices for tapping into creativity by shifting thinking toward productive new definitions about what is possible in life.

Chapter 14: Now What?

Ehrenreich, Barbara. *Living with a Wild God: A Nonbeliever's Search for the Truth about Everything*. New York: Grand Central Publishing, 2014.
Raised an atheist and rationalist, trained as a scientist, Dr. Ehrenreich's memoir recounts her quest—beginning in childhood—to find "the Truth" about the universe and the meaning of life.

Houston, Jean. *The Search for the Beloved: Journeys in Mythology and Sacred Psychology*. New York: Tarcher, 1997.
Sacred psychology assumes that the deepest yearning in every human soul is to return to its spiritual source, and this title provides a modern-day structure for this traditional spiritual quest, incorporating personal mythology, "rites of pathos," and archetypal imagery.

Chapter 15: Do My Work

Heermann, Barry, PhD. *Noble Purpose: Igniting Extraordinary Passion for Life and Work*, American Diabetes Association, 2005.
Outlines a positive approach to embrace our work as an adventure and infuse workplaces with meaning and purpose to unlock employee morale, teamwork, and leadership.

Lobenstine, Margaret. *The Renaissance Soul: How to Make Your Passions Your Life*. New York: The Experiment, 2013.
Offers a life-planning strategy for leading a creative, passionate, vibrant, and fulfilling life.

Masters, Robert. *The Goddess Sekhmet: Psycho-Spiritual Exercises of the Fifth Way*. Ashland, OR: White Cloud Press, 2002.
Profound study of the wisdom of Ancient Egypt and, in particular, the powerful Goddess Sekhmet, provided through the lens of contemporary studies in psychology and religion. Includes details about the Egyptian theory of the Five Bodies, as well as Sekhmet's myths, Sacred Names, and rites.

Schucman, Helen. *A Course in Miracles*, Foundation for Inner Peace, 2007.
A complete self-study spiritual thought system consisting of 365 lessons to begin the process to transform one's mind and perceptions.

Wheatley, Margaret J. *Leadership and the New Science: Discovering Order in a Chaotic World*. San Francisco, CA: Berrett-Koehler, 1992.
How new developments in the sciences provide templates for more human-centered, fluid and flexible organizations that can effectively adapt to future changes.

Chapter 16: Sekhmet Rising

Kant, Candace C. *Heart of the Sun: An Anthology in Exaltation of Sekhmet*, (Kindle edition eBook), iUniverse, 2011.
A collection of vast and varied encounters people have had with the Goddess Sekhmet, including prayers, meditations, and poems.

Krasskova, Galina. *When the Lion Roars*. Hubbardston, MA: Asphodel Press, 2011.
Introduction to the venerated Egyptian Goddess, Sekhmet, through a collection of devotional articles, prayers, and other insights from those who honor Her today.

Roberts, Alison, PhD. *Hathor Rising: The Power of the Goddess in Ancient Egypt*. Rochester, VT: Inner Traditions, 1997.
Examines the feminine aspect of Egyptian religion, shedding light on the pivotal role of the Goddess Hathor-Sekhmet.

Tate, Rev Dr. Karen. *Goddess Calling: Inspirational Messages and Meditations of Sacred Feminine Liberation Theology*. Alresford, Hampshire, UK: Changemakers Books, 2014.
Exploring the deities, ideals, and archetypes of the Sacred Feminine.

ABOUT THE AUTHOR

Dr. Helena Judith Sturnick spent her career as a change agent in higher education and organizations in difficulty. She has been the president of five universities and colleges and, in her last presidency, a student residence complex was named for her. She has also served as Vice President and Director of the Office of Women for Higher Education at the American Council on Education in Washington, DC. As a published author and consultant-coach, she has worked in nine countries. Now living in Florida, she still enjoys working professionally, and is continuing her exploration of Supernormal realities.

CPSIA information can be obtained
at www.ICGtesting.com
Printed in the USA
BVOW08s1634270118
506475BV00002B/253/P